It's all Just Rock and Roll...

A Story of one girl's bust up with breast cancer

by

Alex Jagger

ISBN:1533088357

When life gives you lemons a G&T normally follows. When life sets the alarm bells to maximum volume – it's time to listen.

Dedicated to all those whose alarm bells are

ringing.

To Alistair and Miss Daisy, may our bells always be full of sunshine.

Alex

x

Alex Jagger

Acknowledgements

I would like to take this opportunity to thank all those that were a huge part of my story, I couldn't have of done it without you. Especially the two Nessa's, you both travelled cross country to be with me in my hours of need and I made you watch really bad TV, for that I am truly grateful. I was very lucky to have been assigned Una from the Saturdays as my chemo nurse, a true angel sent to save me. Christine, Jayne, Jane and Catriona, you all picked me up off the floor far too many times to count, you listened to me when I barely made sense and you sat with me when talking made me feel sick – you know how much torture that was for a chatter box like me. To everyone that sent me messages, flowers, cards and little treats that were always perfectly timed – you helped more than you will eve know. To Dave, we may be a very unconventional family but you filled my freezer with food, brought me fennel and kept Daisy smiling, for that I am truly grateful. And of course the one and only Miss Daisy, one amazing girl who has been through one crazy time and come out all guns a blazing. I am very proud of her and believe she is full of the very best kind of magic.

And to Alistair, the sunshine I never knew existed. Being with you makes me feel like the luckiest girl in the world.

Alex Jagger

When life gives you lemons a G&T normally follows. When life sets the alarm bells to maximum volume – it's time to listen.

It took a double dose of breast cancer and all that it brings to get me to wake up and smell the finely ground coffee. I was the girl full of self doubt, self loathing and self fulfilling prophecies. I was the career girl, educated girl, mother, wife, (ex actually) friend and all round sociable girl with a hole in my soul of never being quite enough. For what I don't think I really knew.

Until the day when I had the wake up call of all wake up calls. This was the day that changed everything. I did what every girl worth her salt would do. I cried, screamed, shouted, cried some more and then worked out how to keep my head (and my hair) when the rest of the world was going mad. I was the queen of distraction therapy – to avoid anything that might force me to really delve into the pit of despair that was me.

I gave Paris Hilton a run for her money on the shopping front and would have put 60 Minute Makeover to shame with my painting and decorating skills.

You name it, I painted it, bought it, moved it or upcycled it. Feng Shui was my savior, I was convinced that putting the dustbins in the right corner would stop my bank

account being empty at the end of every month and would attract the love of my life. For a girl who worked more than full time hours, had a young daughter and a set of sociable friends, I was busy as a bee in every other waking second.

Alex Jagger

My relationships left a lot to be desired. A side effect of dead parents (I was 15 when that all that started) – needing to belong to someone. I just always chose the wrong 'somcone'. But back then 'someone' was better than no-one. That's not a good look and only serves to diminish confidence and self respect. I believed nothing of myself. I believed I was about to get 'found out', that everyone at work would realise I'm a fraud, that all my friends were only hanging out with me because they felt sorry for me and my husband was ready to rightfully leave. My self talk was a shocker. (By the way, I was great at my job, I was not a fraud, there was nothing to find out, I am a great friend and I left my husband in a moment of lucidity).

Cancer saved me - crazy thing to say really. The pain, the fear and the unknown pushed me towards a strength I didn't know I had. I found my sunshine and worked my socks off to sort out the mess I'd got myself in.

Through my metaphorical boxing match with cancer and all that it brings, I wrote about a journey of a broken girl who found her way, using the most unconventional of methods. That girl was me and this is my story, told as it

happened, written in real time. It is brutally honest and from the heart, it is emotional as much as it is practical as it is funny. I complemented my chemotherapy with natural remedies and tricks to avoid nasty side effects and I worked out a strategy that got me through all eleven of my surgeries in ways that amazed my doctors.

I hope this story gives you inspiration to live your dreams and the belief that things always get better, even when everything seems absolutely hopeless.

Always keep your face towards the sunshine – never hide in the shadows again.

<u>Where it all began.</u>

June 14th 2013

Hello. My name is Alex Jagger, I'm 42, have an amazing 5- year-old daughter called Daisy, am happily back to being a 'Jagger' again in a very grown up way, a self confessed workaholic in a job that I love (and I'm not just saying that incase any from work is reading this),

have some mighty amazing people around me and I have been diagnosed with breast cancer twice in the last 5 months, clearly once wasn't enough for me.

As a girl who needs to be doing stuff most of the time, the prospect of five months of chemotherapy stretching out

ahead of me is a little daunting. Not only for the obvious reasons, but also for the boredom factor, if I'm allowed to think I may be bored through periods of recovery. I figured out that writing about it every day would provide a welcome distraction, as well as give Miss Daisy something to read later in life in case she ever wanted to know about it – Daisy is my daughter – and to stop me online shopping. Who am I kidding, I think online shopping is a must under these kind of circumstances.

This is my story.

The events that have brought me to today, the 14th June 2013.

<u>Diagnosis number 1.</u>

On January 2nd 2013 I was diagnosed with breast cancer. It was on my dad's birthday.

I was hoping that would have been a good omen, but clearly he still wasn't happy with me for having wooden floors and blinds over carpets and curtains, but that's a whole different story about caring things to say on one's death bed. My dad's death bed that is, clearly I have no intention of anything quite so premature.

A few things ran through my head; clearly I was devastated; Daisy could be without me; it doesn't work without me; I was broken by the loss of my mum who died of cancer when I was 15 (she had breast cancer at 42, was history repeating itself); I don't want to break Daisy and the thought of her being without me frankly does not bare thinking   about. In a haze of attention, sympathy and sedation I had to work out how on earth to get through this. So I decided to choose the distraction approach, look at the good out of all of this nonsense and prepare to get better. I have to say, easier said than done, but determination reigned.

Hours felt like day, days like weeks and weeks likes months whilst I was having surgery, waiting for results, more surgery, more results, more tests, more results and the agonizing decisions about my life that I had to make on my own, but I did it and seemed like I was making progress.

I managed to keep the big C away from Daisy. The thought of having to tell her made me cry and ache inside.

Telling her seemed wrong. Through the many agonizing decisions I faced, I chose to decline chemotherapy and opt for radiotherapy. It was a statistics game, not my strong point, so I opted for intuition and my intuition was screaming out at me to not have chemotherapy. I can't

explain this. The torture of not knowing what to do and having to decide on my own. I was single, recently separated from a 10-year marriage. I had friends and family who wanted to help but no one could face that kind of responsibility so I followed my heart. Stupid, perhaps, but at the time there was nothing else I could have done. I challenged the doctors and demanded information about everything to try and do the right thing.

I was relieved that Daisy was spared my pain and I dug very deep to be the happy mum she knew and loved. I'd endured 7 surgeries to chop away cancer ridden flesh so clearly she knew something was up, but the lack of physical change i.e. keeping my hair, meant I could be a little sparing with the medical truth.

Looking back, I have no idea how I got through the dark nights alone, wrestling with what was the right thing to do. I was lucky as my many amazing friends and family did everything they could to keep me going, which they did through distractions and gin. A lot of it.

I hadn't bargained on the mini breakdown that I thought I had quite successfully kept to myself. Clearly I hadn't as it had some stupid consequences. I lost my mind. Well and truly lost my mind. In no time at all I tried desperately to

go back to my 'normal' life. I made my Masters graduation (did I mention I got a distinction), got myself a swanky new job and started 6 weeks of radiotherapy, all in the same week.

Some said brave, I say stupid.

Here We Go Again

On a fine Sunday morning in May just as my radiotherapy was coming to an end, I was at home, had my best buddy and her daughter staying. I was in the bathroom and I stumbled on the annoying slate tiles on the floor. As I steadied myself my hand landed on my left boob. Something felt a little odd.

I felt a little silly even thinking anything sinister was in there, I mean, I was just coming to the end of 6 weeks of radiotherapy, I'd had a million scans on both boobs, all was clear only 5 months ago.

But there it was, clear as anything.

A lump.

I woke Nessa up and made her feel it to make sure I wasn't going mad and yep, it was there.

That Sunday was a tad surreal. I took Daisy to her Dads, had a good cry about it then came home, randomly picked up a trampoline for my sister who lives in Cornwall and then went to see a film. I can't even remember what it was, I am sure Nessa will remind me as I chose it, so it will have been rubbish by her standards, in fact I think her and Ro were texting all the way through it.

Three days later I was back at the hospital with my surgeon and 6 days later, I had my last radiotherapy treatment in the morning then went into surgery in the afternoon to remove lump number 2. Of course I worked all the way through this – stupidity reigned supreme all over again.

Thank goodness for annoying slate bathroom tiles.

Diagnosis Number 2

On 29th May 2013 I was told I had breast cancer again.

This was serious and very, very scary. I don't really remember the day apart from snippets. I inappropriately launched myself at my surgeon in a bid to hug him - which looking back was very funny - after having very serious conversations about chemotherapy, mastectomies, full body CT scans and imminent surgery,

rather than shake his hand I clung onto him. After all this was going to be the man who was going to save me, I felt wholly appreciative for his urgency and respect for my woeful situation.

I'm not sure one person has seen so many different emotions from me in such a short space of time, from crying whilst coming out of my anesthetics, to launching myself at him, making him laugh with my very inappropriately timed jokes to making him tell me if he likes my hair whilst lying naked from the waist up as he's checking my scars. To be fair to me, my hair had all just been chopped off in preparation for the inevitable and I had got so used to my boobs being an object of illness that being a chatterbox whilst dealing with supremely difficult situations was the only way I knew how.

That crazy day ended with some sedation. My sister out me to bed. I was alone, had cancer again, believed my time had come and that history had in fact done its worse. I thought I was going to leave Daisy at the tender age of 4. She wouldn't have remembered me. My heart was broken.

What do you do now?

I didn't remember the days that followed. I clung onto Daisy at any given opportunity in the run up to me having to tell her what was happening. I spent most of my time being prepped for treatment and having every scan that I think has ever been invented.

The good news was all my scans came back clear and the surgery to remove my lymph nodes also reported that the cancer had not spread.

PHEW!

So I saw Mr. Usman (my surgeon) a lot, I saw Wendy, my breast care nurse a lot, I saw my oncologist, I was booked in for a mastectomy and reconstruction surgery for after my chemotherapy.

I told work, I told my friends, I made a whole load of people cry. After all, cancer the second time around never really sounds that good. I went to Daisy's school to tell them, I told all her friends parents. And then it was time to tell Daisy. One of the hardest things I have ever had to do.

Dave had found some books to help us know what to say. I didn't like any of them. No-one really had any advice on how to tell her, but then why would they. So I went for the direct approach. If you know me, there is no surprise there.

What followed was heart breaking. Daisy punched me repeatedly and then cuddled me so tight, almost like she was trying to crawl back inside me, to where it was safe and warm. Her biggest issue was with my hair. My hair was long; it was about to be cut short in readiness for me to lose it.

And then, we just all got on with it.

I had my hair cut short, bought a wig and got organized for what was about to come.

Through all of this I had serious moments of imminent death. I really thought I was in trouble. This coupled with moments of huge elation which I can't really explain. I was completely overwhelmed at the love and care people showed. It was clear that I had some truly amazing people around me who I couldn't have done any of this without, and luckily they wanted to get me through. Phew! (Again)

And Breath.....

I Made a Choice

I was a super busy person. It turns out for more reasons than just the normal stuff, but that's another story. I had 18 weeks of chemotherapy stretching out in front of me and I was at a loss of how I was going to get through it. I had heard all sorts of stories about the horrors of chemo and I was scared. I had felt fated to die from this, isn't this what I had always feared, I am my mother's daughter after all.

So, I made a choice. I was always going to be my mother's daughter, but I was not going to die in the same way. My daughter was far too young to be without me, she needed me to teach her about how amazing

life is and what incredible things we can all do.

I had my own dreams to fulfil, things to do and people to meet. There is no way this was going to get the better of me.

I researched what to do, how to get through this in the best possible way so that at the end of the chemo and surgery I was going to be a better person in spite of the traumas I was currently facing. I was clearly giving myself a metaphorical high five at this point and was ready to take on the world.

Part of my success was to be keep a diary about my journey. For me, to keep me sane and possibly stop a touch of online shopping, for Daisy in case she ever wanted to know and for those that wanted to see how I was doing without having to ask. One thing I have learnt, is that people have no idea what to say to someone who is facing what I am.

Friday 14th June 2013 6pm.

Just had a call from the Healthcare at Home people, as I am having chemo at home. A very quick cheery conversation, we could have been talking about booking a restaurant for dinner next week it was that cheery, but we were arranging my chemo. It starts on Wednesday next week!

Five days' time. EEK!

This feels a little bit real now. I had put myself in a nice happy mental state where I had temporarily forgotten

why I didn't go to work today, why I had my hair cut short and why I have been doing a very good impression of a 60-minute makeover house programme with my new collection of lamps and cushions and painted feature walls, all painted at around 4am. I'm exhausted but can't sleep. Decorating has kept my inner scary voice at bay in those horrible witching hours.

Hang on - it's because I've got grade 3 aggressive breast cancer in both breasts now- how on earth can I forget.

It's time to put my boxing gloves on and power on through the next 18 weeks of chemo and get better. For good. If I am one of the lucky ones and make the 3 weekly cycles by staying as infection free as possible, I'll be finished by 23rd October. I think XFactor will have started by then.

Alex Jagger

<u>Saturday 15th June</u>

Saturday mornings are my favourite mornings of the whole week. It's the morning that Daisy and I stay in bed for ages watching TV, drinking milk shakes and generally talking rubbish. Oh, and this morning she was knitting. She has offered to teach me how to knit when

I'm too poorly to get out of bed, something to look forward to. Now that she is getting her head around what's coming, all done through humor and an ex husband

who has stepped up to the seriousness of the situation and is going all out to help Daisy and to help me in any way he can – all good. So, I have her knitting lessons along with the other treats she has offered up:

- Shining my head when my hair falls out – please note only Miss D can say this and get away with it.
- Reading to me
- Playing games together
- Creative's

All very good things. She doesn't want to sing so much she said. Thank god for small mercy's as she was blessed with the same tuneful voice as her mother.   So this morning was a little sad for me with the knowledge that next Saturday morning I will be 3 days into my first chemo cycle and may not be up for any of our Saturday morning treats. Also sad as it's becoming very apparent that Daisy is a little bored with her mummy's sore boobies (her words). Even the fact that I now have matching bright blue sore boobies is not doing the trick.

They are blue, not because I thought it a good ploy to entertain my daughter as that would be a little weird, but because when having lymph nodes removed you have the joy of having a radioactive injection through

your nipple that provides a guide to the order

of the lymph nodes. Through surgery blue dye is injected in to make sure they are removed in order to see if the cancer has spread and how far. It's one of the most painful injections I've had and I've had 2 of them.

The dye stays for months. The first time Daisy found it really funny and it helped her remember I was sore on that side, this time she's so over it. So even though I'm so sore from surgery still and I have this odd pins and needles thing going on in my back where the nerve has been cut, she's a little pissed off that she can't throw me around like she used to. All her class at school also know I have blue boobs – I know this for many reasons but mainly because I have never had so much attention whilst picking her up.

So to try and put some time perspective in Daisy's head we had a good chat this morning about my chemo and we've agreed on a lot of hand washing and generally how I may be for the next few months. We talked about the things we can do together at home and when I mentioned that by Christmas I will be a lot better with chemo over and the first big surgery done, she immediately got out her pen and paper and started writing her Christmas list.

Anyway, I've had my fresh cancer fighting juice, Jason Vale eat your juicy heart out, and I'm off to make the most of this day, the sun is shining and as Nina Simone says, it's a new dawn, it's a new day, it's a new

life for me and I'm feeling good! I may retract that statement in the coming days by the way!

Sunday 16th June 2013

Sunday mornings, in complete contrast to Saturday mornings, are frantic from the minute Daisy and I wake up. I'm not entirely sure why really as nothing happens until 9am so why on earth we are flying around the house at 6am is still beyond me, but we still do it. Daisy is with Dave on Sundays so we need to be ready by 9am and Daisy is always really excited. Dave comes round, we have a coffee and always have a chat these days and then off they go to have a great day what ever they end up doing. We all need our routines and I've really realised how much Daisy does, so keeping things as normal as they can be in all of this is really important for her.

I am very impressed at how Dave and I have handled this whole break up stuff, again another story but a very grown up one that we both should be mighty pleased about as it could have been very different.

It is clear how much my cancer has effected him, not just as Daisy's mum but as a friend and the woman

he was married to for 10 years. I can sometimes see the pain in his eyes when he looks at me, as I can when most people   I know look at me at the moment and that's OK.

I'm on the other side of this evil disease for the first time (well second but you know what I mean) and have been touched by a number of other people's reactions.

I think I thought that I wasn't really that important to people (ever the doubter) but I can very proudly say that I now know I am to some. And if there was a competition for how many grown men and women one person can make cry or render speechless, I would win hands down. Even the breast care nurse at hospital last week was completely speechless with me when I told her what had been happening, surely she was trained to know what to say. Cue inappropriate joke, always works in these situations.

So, Daisy has taken to wearing a doctor's coat over the last few days with hand gel in one pocket, finger knitting in the other (very important) and a stethoscope around her   neck.

It doesn't take a genius to work out that she is also preparing herself for my forthcoming treatment by making sure she has clean hands all the time and the fact she just wants to look after me. I find it amazing how she is processing all this huge information by playing the doctor role.

She has fixed all of her toys and now she wants to fix me. And she will, along with the chemo that is. But I am so relieved that she is ok talking about what may or may not happen to me and how we can all get through it together, so

her playing the doctor is working. It's much better than her initial reaction of laughing uncontrollably, punching me in my scar and then crying holding me so tightly it was as if she was tying to get back inside my womb. She's doing very well so far.

I have 3 days left before chemo starts and I am starting to get a bizarre nesting feeling, like the one you get before the birth of a child when you want everything to be done right, clean and ready. I can't quite believe I am comparing chemo to having a baby. The prize at the end is slightly different but equally as amazing, they both involve a new life.

I have a shopping list, for those that know me this is not unusual, but a slightly different list this time   involving incredibly boring things but things that will get me through the next few months of side effects.

 I did read yesterday that Mulberry handbag sales are in decline for the first time since the recession began, I'm not saying I propped up their sales or anything, but they are not on my shopping list any more. You do the math's, as they say.

I have things such as:

Mouthwash to ease mouth ulcers; Eye drops to ease sore eyes when eye lashes fall out as they will run with no lashes to stop it; Nice soft tissues as when all hair falls out; all hair you don't see does such as nose hair that would stop your nose from running normally; Nice moisturizer to stop dry skin; Fresh fennel and apples, I read that one person juiced fennel and apples every day and she claimed it stopped her hair from falling out. I am making the assumption if that was the case it would be big news and everyone would be doing it, but I don't care, I'm going to do it anyway, along with all the other fresh fruit and veg that I'm going to place repeat orders for.

I have found certain juicing recipes that help build immune systems and as mine will be severely compromised I'm going to try very hard to do what I can to keep me strong whilst I am being poisoned. So I'm going to force myself to drink every day.

Hand gel so everyone, including myself, can stop the   spread of germs when around me. Although there is a bit of a myth going on with the whole infection stuff. Everyone assumes that I will pick up infections from other people so should keep away from enclosed spaces etc. even the breast care nurse in hospital told me this. My oncologist has told me that its actually infection from myself that will make me ill. The bacteria in my gut that you would never normally be a problem can make me ill through chemo. So I am my own worse enemy. Nothing new there.

Thermometer, one I can actually read! If my temp goes over 38 I have a special number I call and am told if I need to get myself to a hospital or not. Protocols are in place for chemo patients, they are placed in quarantine and given IV antibiotics. I will be doing my best to avoid this as it sounds no fun at all. But on the plus side it means you get your own private room.

A nice soft and cozy blanket. I like this one! Nessa is a girl after my own heart when it comes to finding some comfort in all this and this was her suggestion. And various other things that I apparently need to help ease aching muscles. I get all the anti sickness stuff at the same time as the chemo, so let's see how that works out for me.

So this is my mission for the day as well as to do the big clean in the house, not that I don't ever clean because clearly I do, but I'm going to go to town on the place today. As my house will become a hospital for one day every 3 weeks and my absolute desire to stay as well as I can through this I want to be sure. In fact, I have the next 3 days clearly planned with as many distractions as I can possibly fit in. So by Wednesday morning I will be ready for what ever is going to happen to me.

How bizarre, waiting to be ill! Apart from recovering from the five operations I've had in the last 5 months, which I've   done remarkably well,

I have not been ill at all. Yes, clearly I've got cancer, I'm not in denial. But I've not actually felt ill. Quite the opposite really as I have taken juicing fruit and veg very seriously and have probably been the healthiest I've ever been. How very ironic.

Just before I go on my cleaning and shopping mission, a few things I learnt yesterday:

- When painting walls, use the same type of paint as was used before, i.e. matt paint on matt paint. I did some midnight painting again last night and this morning I just have shiny satin paint on matt. Silly
- When talking to people for the first time about this, to stop me becoming a freak show and no one knowing what to say to me,

just say something, anything as nothing will offend me. But please don't ignore it as that's a little weird! I saw someone the other day I hadn't seen since having may hair cut short and they didn't mention it! I had to say it myself as its so clear its short! That same person held a whole conversation with me the day after I was diagnosed with cancer, which they knew, about stuff and didn't mention it! I so know how hard it is and this is no criticism, its just so hard for people sometimes as they think my reaction could be so adverse (it never is by the way). The more open the better. Sometimes there are no other words than this is just rubbish. It is and it's fine to just say that.

- Short hair sticks up so much in the morning, its quite amazing! I'm not complaining, when I'm bald as a badger I will be longing for sticky up hair.
- Hearing from people who have read my words has been one of the most surprisingly helpful things so please carry on as its helping me get through.
- I love love love my friends and family.

My mop and bucket beckon.....

Monday 17th June 2013

Somebody now really needs to confiscate my paint brushes. I am running out of things to paint so found myself painting something already painted, just a different colour. My mission yesterday was to shop and clean. Not paint.

Shopping, I am very good at, but to my disappointment the items on my list were not overly exciting. All purchased now, except the nice soft blanket. It was pointed out by a number of people that if I added some more satisfying purchases, such as shoes my shopping trip may have been more fulfilling. I figure I wont be going out on the town for a few months and I do have a very impressive shoe collection already (when has that ever stopped me) so I had method in my madness as surely it's appropriate to have a "I've just finished chemo' treat to look forward to in October.

I did of course forget hats, not something I have now, but I intend to start a little collection! The best bit about the whole shopping trip was driving there and back. I have the best company car, now. Firstly, thank you to Andre for deciding he didn't want it any more and to James for letting me change it. I love it! The only problem is when I'm on my own all I do is cry when I'm driving. Random really and not sure what happens to me when I get going, but it really wasn't the look I was going for. Much better when Daisy is in it with me as all we do it sing, very very badly.

Cleaning I really don't like, one of those necessary things in life that I just don't like. However, I found it quite satisfying this time around and now my house feels ready to rock and roll on the chemo front. Clearly though, I do not.

Painting has seemed to keep the fear at bay, no idea why. It all started when I found a Feng Shui book one night when   I couldn't sleep. I decided to go straight to the 'health' section and when looking at my house and where that was, I realised it was full of clutter. I then moved to the relationship section and found an overflowing rubbish bin, no wonder I thought. I moved through each section and literally de cluttered the entire house over night. Clearly I am clutching at straws here, but I'll give anything a go!

I would be the envy of any house make over programme as I have gone through each room at a demon

pace and have become an expert in lighting and cushions! Distraction at its best, especially now.

So, 2 days to go until chemo starts. Lots going on today and tomorrow getting ready for the big day. I am having a cold cap system installed for the duration of the treatment. The idea being, you wear the cold cap before the treatment starts and for the duration of the treatment and it cools down the hair follicles and gives you a 50/50 chance of a reduction in hair loss. Yes, I know I am willing to try anything, that is along with the fresh fennel and apple juice to drink every day. It will either work, or not. But I won't know unless I try and as it's all part of the home care service it would be rude not to really.

Then I have my pre assessment with blood test etc. and a full brief of what happens when I have the treatment and what to expect during and after. It does feel so strange waiting to be ill. I have tried to compare how this feels in a number of different ways:

It's a little bit like going on holiday, well, not at all as I'm not going anywhere nice or tropical, but that feeling of wanting to make sure you have everything you need and everything is packed etc.

Its like having a baby, bag packed and nervous about   how much its going to hurt (a lot by the way) and is the baby going to be ok after etc.

It's like having surgery, the anticipation of the pain you   may feel, but again not at all as you get the best ever happy drugs to go with it. And I am still working on the assumption that the last anesthetist turned down my request for a home service of happy drugs every 3 weeks throughout the chemo cycle. I asked if he would pop round. I think it was a no.

That's all I've got. In reality it's like something I have never known. I'm working on the theory that the anticipation may be worse than the actual event and if I work on a worse case scenario basis anything better is a bonus.

Tuesday 18th June 2013

Big news today, well not quite as big as the news I have been delivering to people over the last few weeks, but all the same, for me, big news. I did not paint anything last night.

I know!

So, chemo tomorrow, my last day of anticipation and wonder of what's to come. My last day of this particular chapter in my life as it's nearly time to get my boxing gloves firmly in place to get myself through this craziness. Wishing time away has become a nasty phrase in my mind now, but I really would like to fast forward just a little, even just the first cycle to see what I'm up against.

I have learnt a massive amount about myself over the last few weeks and there is one thing for sure, when I know what I'm up against I can deal with it, what ever that may be. I say that now. Throughout my mini cancer breakdown that was not the case. I had my head so firmly in a place where the sun doesn't shine that no manor of logic, knowledge or any thing to be honest would have helped. But that was then, and this is now.

I've never had such clarity. Talk about being stripped back to nothing and revealing the true me. It is said that people show their true colour's when really up against it, its fair to say I've been up against it. Should I feel vulnerable? I have felt so unbelievably vulnerable, especially earlier in the year, I did not know how to deal with what was happening, so probably didn't. But for now, my vulnerability has morphed into a whole lot of determination to live. I don't mean   that dramatically. Although facing one's own mortality not once but twice has been a little tricky. I mean that in terms of I am determined to be happy, healthy, have lots and lots of fun and I am really not going to get hung up on nonsense. Oh and I also want to make the world happy and some people in it. Is this the point that I go on about world peace, I wonder?

There's a famous quote by Marilyn Monroe and in it she says

'if you can't handle me at my worst then you sure as   hell don't deserve me at my best' now

 I am sure she was meaning her massive insecurities and out of control'ness. I am not - well not entirely as I believe I have displayed those at times - I know hard to believe.

So back in the real world, my plan for the day. Before that, if I become really annoyingly positive and start quoting all sorts of people, and believe me I really could, someone please tell me to stop. Back to today. Cope with the flurry of activity that I think will happen with nurses and equipment and information. Watch those around me get their heads around what they are up against whilst I may melt away into a much nicer world in my head. I've become very good at that. It's fair to say I am very, very scared about what's coming, but if I try and get all Stephen Covey about it, I need to start with the end in mind. The end being a very healthy, happy me. With hair and boobs of some description - a reality what I melt away and think about, that's a good focus.

I also need to go shopping, again. I looked in the fridge this morning and realised there wasn't anything in it apart from fruit and vegetables, all very good but if I remember back to morning sickness days, and times that by some, then there is no food in there I will want to eat, and I must eat to   keep strong and fend off infection. I will of course be having my juiced fresh fennel daily whilst wearing a cold cap, not that I am desperately trying to keep my short (sticky up) hair, its better than none.

Yesterday, some good things happened:

My big boss thought I was 33! 'Forget the cancer, you wear well' Made my day.   Hang out with those that bring out the best in you, I did and it was good, again it made my day.

I've had so many people letting me know about my words, I've loved it and it's helping more than you can possibly know. Again, made my day.   I realised about all the money saving elements of this treatment:

- no waxing required

- no shampoo/conditioner and all other hair related   stuff

- no mascara needed (I'm really gutted about that; I do   have good eye lashes)

Hold your breath! In the news yesterday, apparently a new

study has shown that if breast cancer patients hold their breath it helps.... If only I had known!   On news and studies about breast cancer, which I have become a bit of an expert on recently. Over the last couple of weeks in the news there was a question over the benefit of mammograms, as in, they are not as good as was once thought. Please can I just say that although I found both of my lumps myself, I spent 30 days going to hospital having radiotherapy along with a lot of other women. I, for some reason, was a magnet for people to come and talk to me, in fact I knew so many of other peoples stories it was a bit ridiculous. But every other woman who spoke to me told me their breast cancer had been detected through mammograms, honestly, everyone. So please take that particular news story with a pinch of salt.

I learnt throughout that experience that no manor of diversion tactics stopped people talking to me. I learnt all about all types of cancer. I did not want to. But at times I thought people thought I was there just to be talked to, I'm sure it was a shock when my name was called and I went for my own treatment. I looked a picture of glowing heath when everyone else looked grey and pissed off.

<u>June 18th 2013</u>

Someone somewhere clearly needs me to finish painting my house as my treatment has been put back to Thursday.

NO NO NO! was my response on the phone call. The poor nurse Helen didn't know what to say. I can add her to my long list then.

I always think things happen for a reason. I'm struggling with why my nervous system is being messed with on   this occasion:

- To finish painting, I can do that when I'm feeling good
- Shopping, I'm bored of shopping, my god did I just say that!

That's all I've got! It's so they can spend more time with me apparently. Fair enough. What's another day, well about a week in my head.

And Breath!

<u>June 19th 2013</u>

The rattling of my central nervous system yesterday was short lived, thankfully. After I got over the shock of having to wait another day for this apparent horror to start, my chemo nurse, Una, arrived for my pre assessment. We have affectionately named her Una from The Saturdays!

She doesn't know this of course, but it will only be a matter of time before I call her that. She is lovely, as you would expect from a chemo nurse and she managed to make me feel very calm quite quickly, which I believe is a little tricky with me.

So, my chemo is called FEC. I have called it many things that I couldn't possibly put into print, but I am quite happy that there seems to be a little humour in the name at least. Una from The Saturdays went through all my possible side effects and what I need to do about them, if I get them. She really did make me feel like it won't be as bad as I think it will be, but I am working on a worse case scenario so that any thing better is a bonus. She said a number of times that the drugs I'm given really do help me get through. Well in just over 12 hours I'll find out.

11.30am tomorrow is time to get my boxing gloves firmly in place.

So Una from the Saturdays took some blood, got me to sign a load of consent forms, apparently I had done the bulk of them with the Oncologist, I actually can't remember doing   any. Then she left. Nessa (BF) was with me and we both looked at each other and realised that we had a free day, a day with now nothing else to do and no one to see and with no children between us.

So here was my treat for the day that I so needed, a day out with Nessa! The day was like a gift and was just what I needed, but just didn't realize it! A day that I didn't need to do anything cancer related or chemo related and that didn't involve painting. We got the train into Shrewsbury and went out for a very nice late lunch in the sunshine. A couple of glasses of the most wonderfully tasting wine set us both up for a day of laughing. A lot. At everything. A few very good things came out of this day.

It worked. I was in bed by 7.30pm and slept for 12 hours. I slept for the first time since December 9th 2012 when I found my first lump.

This morning I woke up bright eyed and bushy tailed, made my magic green smoothie packed full of goodness and completely forgot what I was doing.

I actually felt like Nessa and I were on holiday. We have been on holiday a lot together in the past, in fact we were built to go on holiday together.

The phone rang, it was Daisy wanting to see me, fantastic I thought, a very big treat as she's been at Dave's so wasn't expecting to see her. A little knock on the door and Daisy comes in and clamps herself to me for half an hour before school, hugging me so tight it felt delicious.

Chemo tomorrow.

June 21st 2013

Oh boy, yesterday was a very tricky day but I think it was going to be regardless. It started having not had much sleep, to Daisy also not coping with what the day was going to bring either, so that kept me very occupied until she went to school, lots of talking about this bloody thing called cancer and why I had to have this treatment, but she left happy, phew!

My sister Nessa had arrived in the early hours; I knew that as she posted a picture of the sunrise by my house on Facebook which I saw before I woke her up. Crazy driving through the night from Cornwall, but she was here so all good.

So I got in the shower, washed my hair and realised that this was the last time I will be able to wash my hair the same for about 7 months, I will of course be able to wash my hair just differently to stop it falling out. Things I will do for vanity.

Tears streamed down my face as I clocked my blue boobs and all my scars and the fact that I have not had anything 'normal' since December 18th, the day of my first surgery. Since that day my world was different and has continued to change, and here we are today, the first day of my chemo and washing my hair differently.

I couldn't speak for crying and that lasted right up to Una from the Saturdays arriving. She has an amazing ability to calm me down, but she has been doing this for 23 years. I confessed about her new nick name to her and she liked it which was a good.

So, it will come as no surprise that I had redecorated a whole room just to have my treatment in. The theory being that I can then completely redecorate it again when my treatment is over to take away any memories of the treatment itself.

Chemo association is very common, such as smells   or music so I have put away all my favourite smelling things and will listen to different music throughout. I did though have James Bond ready to watch, I'll never go off James Bond.

In my quest to keep my hair, the cold cap machine was on and ready. This is only available to private patients and as I am lucky enough to be one of those because of work I can have it. I vaguely remember last night getting on my high horse a little about this as it really should be available to everyone.

Hospitals can have them at no cost as there is a charity set up to fund them but still, especially in Shropshire, they wont take them. That makes no sense. It's the one side effect that everyone says is the most distressing, the one that shows to the world you have/had cancer. The company who 's machine I have, called Paxman, have an e petition on their web site for hospitals to take these machines so they can be available to everyone, go and sign it, I have. Its www.paxman-coolers.co.uk.

So back to the tricky day. Cold cap was on, strapped into place and turned on. Goodness, brain freeze for 15 minutes, like I was eating a lot of very cold ice cream, but I wasn't. I got myself in the zone and got through the painful bit whilst it was getting to temperature and then got used to it. I would put a picture up of what it looked like, but as I looked like something out of doctor who, I'll keep that one to myself.

Although I could see Nessa itching to take a picture as she was sat with me, really itching to. She did. If that ever makes it on Facebook, there will be words. Whilst this was happening I had my needle thing put in, my arm wrapped in an electric blanket and had my anti sickness meds, some through the IV and some tablets, again those are only available to private patients as they are too expensive for the NHS, this all seems wrong for this type of toxic treatment.

And we were off. Red drugs first, these are the worst and make all your hair fall out and sick. They act fast - they are in, do what they do and then are flushed out, starting the same day. The next one made me go all pre anesthetic, a treat I wasn't expecting. Short lived though but at that time I could have gone to sleep but the weight of my frozen head stopped me. Then the last one that makes your eyes sore and runny. Just under 2 hours and it was all done. PHEW! First treatment done, 5 to go. Now I know what to expect it will be a whole lot better. My head, however, had to stay freezing for a further 2 hours, I was freezing, but James Bond took my mind off it.

Just before Daisy came back from school, my cold cap was off and my hair was frozen. My body was clearly suffering the effects of all these drugs and I needed to lie down, NOW. And then I started to feel really sick. That's not stopped.

So we all got through the night just about, Daisy is struggling with this because I literally can't move around, I am sure this will ease over the next few days. I am OK if I don't move at the moment. This morning I took my cocktail of anti sickness drugs and I don't intend to move much! I am taking the opportunity of my lucidness to write this or I will forget what's happened as I actually can't really remember much of last night. I guess the amount of drugs in my system, the fear and the tiredness all add up to a mighty confused Alex.

My journey to getting better has begun. I had forgotten what I was doing before yesterday, all my favourite people hanging out with me and lots of lovely cards and messages, I honestly had forgotten why I wasn't going to work, why I was in a funny little bubble and what I was waiting for. Well, although I couldn't find my boxing gloves yesterday, I have them firmly in place now to get the hell through this craziness and get to the other side. I will make it, with bells on.

I need to stop now, horizontalness is calling.

June 22nd 2013

Well, I have made it through my first full day and a half of having chemo without too much of a hitch, well apart from the debilitating tiredness and every time I move wanting to be sick. The anti sickness meds have worked as I haven't been and my logic says that as tomorrow I drop one set of meds, the day after another and are only left with 1 set of anti sickness meds until Wednesday as opposed to 5, I must be on the mend.

I have slept beyond sleeping. Every time my head hits the pillow I am gone. Even with Daisy trying her hardest to wake me up for various reasons there has been no chance, Auntie Nessa, I believe has been run ragged.

Now the lovely Gaby has taken her away for fun and frivolity, Daisy that is, not Auntie Nessa. As soon as Gaby left I was asleep. I love my daughter more than I can say but it's been very tough having her here seeing me like this and not being able to do anything she wants to do. Our Saturday morning this week was in stark contrast last week, she wanted her milkshake, the smell of it was making me sick and every time I moved it wasn't working. Poor girl, she was so bored. And a little pissed off that I wasn't playing, understandably.

I have forced myself to eat and drink my fennel and veg juice. Oh my that has been hard. But I figured that if I drink all my veg then it's in me working its magic (hair loss magic remember) and then I am just eating what I can cope with, beans on toast to be precise. I have lost my taste buds and my sense of smell has gone through the roof, it's like a very intense morning sickness but without the appetite for stodge that I had then.

When pregnant with Daisy, I used to eat a Pizza Hut deep pan pepperoni and mushroom pizza on the way home   from work every day before my tea. And I wonder why I got a little tubby back then.

I've not even had time to be emotional. I'm too busy stopping myself feeling sick. But I do know that I have started this crazy journey and am one down already.

If I keep on getting better each day, then at least I know what I'm up against next time and as long as I stay as free from infection as I can then I know what to do. And there are no more surprises, I know what happens with all the chemo drugs, all the meds and how much I need to zone out with the frozen head for four and a half hours each time, but that's all it is in the grand scale of things. Nothing if it stops my hair from falling out completely.

I also know how long it is before it all starts hitting me and soon I will know how long it lasts. See. Sorted. I have also had so many messages from people that it's kept me going and has been lovely, so thank you. And of course I couldn't have got through without Nessa, no words currently describe how grateful I am. Plus, the box set of James Bond Movies arrived at my door today, I'll be taking him to bed with me when I can handle the noise of TV, I'm hoping that will be tomorrow.

I did wake up earlier, Daisy having fun with Bella,   Nessa probably catching up downstairs on bits and bobs and I lay in bed thinking how funny it was that everyone was carrying on their day to day lives, just getting on with their stuff, having fun, or not, being with people they care about, or not or just generally getting on with stuff without thinking about anything.

I wonder if it's just me that's contemplating life with such vigor at the moment. Feeling massively grateful for the amazing people around me that have literally dropped everything to be at my side and those that have been there through messages, amazing really. And feeling like my life has become an open book for the future, who knows what awaits. Through my mini cancer breakdown, I refused to talk about this to pretty much anyone, look at me now. Try and stop me.

My plan for the rest of the day is to have some time out of bed now the madness of the house has calmed down and I know everyone is ok and having fun. And then beans on toast and sleep. Told you my life was just rock and roll. Maybe one day.

June 23rd 2013

Well, I'm up and writing, wasn't expecting this today   as feeling a bit rough. I stopped a set of meds today and boy can I feel it. Just goes to show what they are doing when you are taking them. BUT so far I have done well. Tired and feel sick and slept for Britain, if that's what this week means in every 3 then bring it on.

Last night I had the most time awake I've had since Thursday, and what did I do? I firstly watched the judges on

The Voice kill my current favourite song (Daft Punk Get Lucky) and then I think I watched most of the absolutely shocking show.

There is one thing about going through this nonsense I am going through, no concentration. I think I have had just about enough concentration to get through the diagnosis and treatment x 2 etc. and it leaves none for anything else, this has been the case mainly from January. But it's ramped up a notch as I haven't been able to watch anything from start to finish, no films yet or programs with much noise. All it's been is Friends and The bloody Voice. I admit my choice of TV programs isn't always the best anyway, Columbo at the top of the list and give me an action film over any other kind and I'm happy. Sadly, I can't cope with them right now. Wont be long I'm sure.

So I slept after The Voice and was rudely awoken by road and train works outside the house at around 3am. It was more like a massive machine was trying to move my house to   a different location, the house was shaking and everything, very bizarre!

But it kept me awake for ages, even the birds singing didn't mask the noise! But I floated off again into the land of sleepy things and had some bizarre dreams. This is the first time I have remembered my dreams since Thursday, and I always have eventful dreams.

It was a work dream telling everyone to follow their instincts and go with what ever works. Yeah! Yeah, I can hear you say! At least Terence Trent

Derby didn't feature. Where he came from in my head who knows. Or Danny from The Script, they have both been in my dreams recently.

So my plan for today, I have eaten. I have ventured onto scrambled eggs and toast and fresh veg and fennel juice, I can't taste anything at all but I know I need to get some goodness inside me to work its magic. I have slept more. I am happy that Daisy will be partying hard at a dinosaur disco soon and having lots of fun, as she did last night with Bella, life saver! And then my plan is to go back to bed and then later eat and then sleep.

SO ROCK AND ROLL!

June 24th 2013

Big news, on the scale of things anyway. Five days in to this chemo nonsense and last night I was up for about 5 hours. Whoop Whoop! It seems my roughness got better as the day went on, after a lot of sleeping that is and some mighty tasty food. I strayed from my safe beans and eggs and ventured into broccoli, bacon and pasta!

I have again dropped another set of anti sickness meds today, the last set from 5 to 1 in 5 days so logic says I'm on the mend.

So today I have been a bit more with it from the word go which is the first time, still can't move too quickly, but hey, who needs to right now. The consequence of my alertness last night was putting Nessa through some serious poor telly watching! I made her endure a film, 17 Again which was on TV, Zach Efron, easy on the eye and that's about it, but still I made her watch the lot and then Marple, oh dear. Sorry! But it's all I could handle as it was easy watching at its best, oh and the volume was down so much as I can't handle much noise, we couldn't actually hear it anyway, that's love for you.

So, we got talking. I haven't really talked much since Thursday, that's a shock in itself, but I have been poorly for the first time physically since having cancer so I have had all on getting myself through the last few days. But last night I was more alert and with it and a little emotional. When I was downstairs yesterday I kept seeing a vision of my sister caring for her little sister with cancer and it was really odd. A vision I am sure neither of us ever wanted to see but it was really happening.

I don't have cancer anymore though, please remember that, it's been cut out, this treatment is to make sure the pesky stuff hasn't escaped and then the surgery will finish it off anyway, so all good.

For one I am not used being cared for,as in I am a very determined person, and am very used to being very independent and doing things for myself and Daisy.

This has not been possible over the last few days as   I haven't been able to make any food on account of not being able to stand for long etc. and just the thought of it making me feel sick. I have of course been able to get myself to bed and to the bathroom as long as I move very slowly, but really, that's it. I have been at the mercy of another to help me get through the day.

So then we got talking about how having cancer has effected me and her and those around us. It's a funny thing, not really in the ha ha sense, just it takes people so differently and puts perspective into most situations, for me anyway. I think I maybe understood for the first time what an impact this is having on so many things and people. It was as if the earth moved on its axis last night as there was sure a seismic shift in my feelings and attitudes towards so many things and I feel like I lie awake last night putting it all into place. I actually did as well! But hey, I am the biggest believer in something good has to come out of tricky situations and that things happen for a reason. I am still struggling with any reasons for this, but I am getting there on getting some good outcomes for my life, and other peoples lives through out this journey and when this chapter moves onto a one with no cancer, treatment or blue boobies!

Don't worry I will not be going on about all my revelations, I will however share my feelings a bit, so I don't forget! I realised, more than ever, that we are all responsible f

or our own happiness, well being and success, with the exception of our children. Our responsibility for them is to show them the joy of independence and allow them to be themselves, knowing they will always have our unconditional love and support. But as adults the beauty surely is to be around those who want to be around you and vica versa. Certainty is captivating. One day when I am a part of someone's world, it will be because it's out of want and not need with lots of good feelings, never negative, it all makes up the big picture. And the very strong desire for me make those I love happy and feel good is very overwhelming! This may sound very basic and very obvious, but it has taken me this long I think, and having cancer or a clear head, or both to see it this clearly. History does not have to repeat itself, and I believe I am in control of that. Oh and I want to go to Hawaii when all this is over!

So my mind has started working again. Should   I apologise now for what might happen in my lucid days through my treatment, or really just go with it. Well, I am looking on the bright side of these 3 weekly cycles and am really hoping that I get some good days out of this towards the end of each cycle to get out more. It might just

help with all this life contemplation, it's exhausting.   So my plan for today is to sleep a little bit more ready   for Daisy's return from school, I really want her to see me up and about

this time. And then I will be forcing magic fennel and veg juice down me with some more tasty food. Who knew it could be so revelatory, and tiring all at the same time! Oh and I might let Nessa watch something good on TV later!

25th June 2013

Typical Alex Jagger behavior crept in yesterday, a glimmer   of energy and a bit of normal thinking and I try too hard to do too much. Bugger!

I completely wiped myself out. And when I say do too much, I mean move around the house a bit, take advantage of Daisy being here, you know, nothing! Just goes to show what this stuff is doing to me. For those campaigning against shocking TV programmes, Nessa watched whatever she wanted last night on account of me being in bed!   So this morning, day 6, I woke up from a frightful dream, more of that later. The best bit was I woke up on my   own. That doesn't sound right either, but what I mean is Daisy slept in her own bed all night last night, get the fan fare out, this is monumental and so needed.

Bribery was exchanged at bed time, but none the less, she did it! At around 6.30am I heard the little pitter patter of feet run, more like screech in to my room and the biggest smile greeted me, with 'mummy, I did it! Do I get

my treat now!' Well, yes of course she does, but the biggest treat this morning was our normal Saturday activities just on a Tuesday. She had milkshake, I had tea and we sat in bed and chatted until it was time to get up for school, for her clearly. Dare I say it was nearly a normal morning.   So a good start to the day.

I have now been on only one set of anti sickness meds for the last 2 days and all has been good, apart from the massive lack of energy of course. This is something that will frustrate the hell out of me and all those around me. There is one thing about me that I am very aware of, my ability to do stuff, doing is the key word here! I am the girl who single handedly redecorated my house in   a matter of days and Feng Shui'd it over night so what am I going to do with no energy and 17 more weeks of   treatment? I'm a little concerned. Let's hope week 3 brings a bit more energy. Please!

Last night I went into the deepest of sleeps, really early. I am amazed I can sleep this much. Someone said to me last week that I just need to sleep through the first week and I remember thinking that would be nice but I really can't see it happening. I eat my words!

My dreams took on a whole new dimension! Gangster warfare is all I can describe it as. Well, a lot of dead people, some had killed themselves and others were just dead. A lot

of very flash fast cars with   massive computers inside them, very posh green and gold doors and then a spidery crab thing that kept following me around until I smoothed it out and it stopped! But I had this over riding feeling as I was waking up that I was dead. I've not shaken it all morning.   Clearly I am not dead, and I have no intention of being, just yet anyway.

Throughout this whole scenario I've not truly believed this might be the end of the road for me. Yes of course the feeling has come and gone, but knowing I don't have cancer any more as it's all been cut away and all this treatment is precautionary' stuff - there is no way I am giving in to this, absolutely NO WAY!

But one thing that has become plain as day is this is changing my life and it won't ever be the same again.

And Breath...

I am taking the dead people in my dream to mean death of situations by the way, I am not in any way a morbid   person. And actually I got to drive the dead people's cars and they were all very flash ones, peach in colour though, which is so wrong.

This much change can't be a bad thing. It may be forced change through my current circumstances, but surely this is

the time to try and do good things when you have time to really think and get it right. Very rarely do we get time when something else isn't taking it up. Granted, I would rather not have had to have cancer to have it, but as I am in this situation, if I make sure I really make a difference and put my demons at bay, then this can be part of my something good coming out of something bad stuff I keep going on about! I always did say I wanted to change the world!

So my plan today, I have had a bath and washed my hair already, I actually think I look almost like me again today, maybe I have all week but I don't think so. I am sat in the garden and the birds are singing, this is the first time I have been outside for the last 6 days. Nessa (BF) is on her way down, Nessa (sister) is frantically keeping me free from infection and hiding food on my plate at every meal to try and get more in me, this is becoming quite funny now! And I plan on doing not a lot, just for a change! I don't want to go for total wipe out again today.

This may be one of the hardest things I will have to conquer throughout this time, learning to not do anything when I really can't.... How is that possible?

26th June 2013

Yesterday was a day of food! Once I started I just did not stop. Something clearly changed yesterday as   I wasn't forcing anything down me as I have been, I wanted to eat, a lot. I was also awake all day. I know that sounds silly. But in the scale of things I have not made a full day awake in the last 7 so things are looking up. I did sleep so well last night that there were no crazy dreams, bit disappointed really. So I am on day 7, 119 days to go until my last treatment. Start with the end on mind and all that!

As I have said, I had a good day yesterday and today has started just as well. In fact, I am actually dressed and feel a little bit more like me again, still a little sensitive, but who wouldn't be with all that toxic stuff pumping through your veins, but I am determined to counteract all that with the pints and pints of raw veg juice I am drinking, and meds of course. On that, I am on my last day of anti sickness meds today, that has to be a good sign.

The Nessa's were en masse yesterday which was just great. Lots of breezing around the house and garden and lots of laughing and eating. And the conversation and thinking turns from self discovery to bikini waxing, which I know far too much about it seems, and all things blusher, sun tan lotion and more waxing.

After much deliberation and a little persuasion, the bet is now on - if I can have chemo then Nessa (BF) can get her waxing done.

No doubt she will be cursing my name mid strip! So now Nessa and I have 2 bets, wig wearing and bikini waxing. Ha!

On hair loss of a different kind, I have been paranoid that my hair is falling out as I am getting funny pins and needles sensations going on. It isn't. It might, but it isn't yet and if it was the feelings in my scalp aren't a sign   my hair is falling out, so I read anyway. Although I am doing what I can to keep the hair on my head, I will of course lose it everywhere else, this is because chemo targets the fastest dividing cells in the body and the hair follicle cells are the 2nd fastest dividing cells we have. There is a chance I'll keep my eyebrows and eyelashes though. I have been very optimistic and bought a new mascara, I can live in hope.

Today it seems I have taken to marmite, what has happened to me, I used to hate it. Not only that but I have been out! Nessa (sister) flew the nest for the day to watch some decent TV probably and Nessa and I thought we were on a road trip! We actually went 20 minutes down the road and to Tesco's, but we did at one point expect to see the sea stretching out ahead of us at the turn of every corner, oh those were the days! Memories came flooding back of our American road trip with promises to do it all again, or was that Glastonbury. Both I think! And of course Hawaii!

So I am pleased to say that today I have been me again, dressed, fully fed and able to

be out and do stuff. And the happy new owner of a real life 4 leaf clover thanks to Cat, now that has to be the sign of a good day!

27the June 2103

It sure is love when your   best buddy declares Brazilian waxing magic is going to happen as a bet to compensate me having chemo!

Sometimes when people have chemo and the inevitable hair loss happens, friends and family cut their own hair off in support. Now I will never let anyone do this, and some have offered, but just NO. I think maybe all my friends need to get Brazilian waxes instead! I actually woke up laughing about this today, this is maybe a sign I need to start getting out a bit more! Anyway, it's a deal and I believe the appointment is being made as we speak!

Is it possible to have a food hangover? If it is, I have one. Boy did I eat again yesterday. I'm not going to every day go on about each and every meal, it's just I'm really impressed that I am eating so well after 1 week. I am craving clean, fresh food only. It sounds silly but I feel like my body is regenerating! In a way it is as all my cells are being killed off and are now starting again, does that mean that my chemical makeup will be different by the end of this? I wonder. I will ask the Oncologist today.

So, I have a visit to Wolverhampton to see my Oncologist. Mr. Blinky eyes I call him, that's not his name clearly, but he blinks so much that you can't really make eye contact very much with him, and I like good eye contact, generally but

especially when talking about things such as me and my future health. I also think he has to brace himself a little when seeing me on account of my incessant questions and challenges. The first time I saw him, the first time I had cancer, I went to see him on my own. Not my smartest move. I was also heading like a juggernaut into my mini breakdown at the time so I really wasn't thinking straight. He even asked me if I was happy to carry on with the meeting with him on my own, I think I dismissed that comment completely and actually remember thinking what a stupid thing to say!   Of course everything he said completely freaked me out and he started giving me all these choices to make. The first time around I had to decide my own treatment as I had caught

it early and the decision was all based on percentages   on recurrence/death over the next 10 years which takes all sorts of factors into account.

If I asked him 1 question I asked him a 100, I took up nearly all his time and did not stop. As it turned out I left, cried all the way home, cried all night and most of the next day. In fact, I probably cried like a very scared person until I had the courage to make the decision.

I did and it was the right one it turned out. But who would have thought 5 months on from that meeting   my recurrence had happened.

If I had accepted chemo the first time around, the second lump would have shrunk but not disappeared. My instinct to not have chemo then has served me well.

Mr. Blinky eyes is, of course, super clever with no   people skills at all. On the last meeting I opened it up by saying to him 'you know it's me, right? I may have changed my name and had all my hair cut off, but its me!' He just said   'YES! You aren't very lucky are you!' I don't care about the no people skills bit and have sort of found my very inappropriate way of being with these people that have my life in their hands.

He knows that I read up about everything, it must be so annoying for him as I really have no idea about anything to do with cancer, apart from my own. I feel like putting together a power point presentation on my toxicity so far and how I have coped with a graph of my temperature and symptoms on an hourly basis with a projection of proposed side effects over the next 17 weeks!

You think I am joking. I wonder if I can go 'Good to Great' on chemo side effects... I do actually have a list of questions for him, I'm sure he can't wait!

I am on day 8, no meds today as I am now flying solo! No meds now until the 11th July when cycle no. 2 starts. Apparently my immune system is at its lowest right now for a few days, hence the temperature checking twice a day and

the aches and pains that are creeping in and out. My poor body. But my concentration is coming back, I watched a whole film last night, and I feel like I can maybe do a bit more stuff. I will try and stop reverting to type and doing too much which I am sure will be very tricky!

So today Nessa (BF) is heading back to Leeds and Nessa (sister) is coming back before heading home. I hate seeing them go but love to see them come back, and just love them full stop! I am sure Cornwall and those there want Nessa (sister) back, not long now I promise! I intend to stop any infection knocking on this door anyway.

We have our trip out to see Mr. Blinky Eyes, that's my road trip for the day! Not quite a trip to Santa Monica Bay or the Big Sur, but it's a trip out! I am in search of the perfect beach by the way, The Big Sur has been the closet so far, it was such a windy day but determined as ever Nessa and I found it, that was a challenge in itself, like the Golden Gate Bridge. A different story.

Once found we stayed on it getting blown around in a bit of a sand storm but it didn't stop us taking in that amazing beach at its best.

We only left it because we were turning into sand sculptures ourselves and I think it was getting a bit painful!

So, power point presentation at the ready and dreaming of The Big Sur. That's my day.

28the June 2013

So my visit to Mr. Blinky Eyes went well, apart from the curve ball he threw me that is. I am doing what I should be doing at the right times so far, so that is good. When I listed my side effects and asked if they were normal, he pointed out that I am in fact on a very intensive treatment programme and that is why I have felt so, well, intensive. I didn't know this before, I actually thought I was on a low dose, I have no idea where I got that from.

Anyway it does explain why I have felt as I have. And anyway again, the good news is my tumour was again oestrogen negative meaning that the chemo is more responsive, hence the high dose, and it means I don't have to have Tamoxifen for 10 years after, PHEW! The growth receptors on my tumour were low which is a good thing, apparently it's the best kind, something about my DNA not being susceptible to fast growing cells and it not being hormone related, I have to say I glazed over a little at this point. It was good news, that's all that mattered, although a little bit of a shock.

The not so good news was it looks like my hair is getting ready to fall out. Bugger! Those pins and needles sensations in my scalp are my hair follicles dying. Looks like Nessa may get away with not having to wear my wig after all! I'll keep cracking on with what I'm doing until it happens though. I do feel like I am trying to hold onto something that I will inevitably lose, which is never good so I guess I can handle having no hair for a few months as it now means   I don't have to take drugs for the next 10 years, when this   is done, it really will be done. No daily reminders, hallelujah!

For once I left one of these horrible appointments laughing and not crying. And then I started talking to Nessa (sister) about why I didn't know it was such an intensive dose. Apart from the obvious fear factor before having it,   Nessa pointed out that I am in fact very intense when in these meetings. Maybe they only say what they think I can handle to get me through the treatment. So I started thinking about this and looked back on all the meetings I have had with all these people, and yes, they have all been very   intense. Intense mainly because I have been given massive news every time that has rocked me to my core, but intense also because I hold eye contact so much as I am trying to take in every word that they are saying, to the point where I am repeating what they are saying in my head as soon as they are saying it to try and take it in. And then I would cry! And then all the questions, boy, not surprised they look a little apprehensive when they see me!

Mr. Blinky eyes was his usual personable self. Not. It was the first time my sister had met him and I could see her trying to work him out in his office, as I was trying my hardest to listen to what he was saying and ask all my questions so I could leave feeling like I knew what I needed to know. I knew at one point she had clocked his wedding ring and was wondering off into the world of what's he's like at home, with his wife. I knew this because its exactly what I had done the last time. We both hoped that he smiled a little more with her! I did though get a laugh out of him but it was very hard work.

So I started thinking about what everyone else is doing, getting on with stuff, going out, driving, working, having fun, getting on planes, going to festivals, getting a Brazilian wax! And I started to feel very jealous. What had I done? Left the house twice in 9 days, whoop whoop! Yes, clearly chemo cancer girl here isn't up for partying, but blimey, now I am feeling more like me again, it was time to test the outside world water. Today, on my own, I got into my very, very lovely car and drove it to the furthest away shops I thought I could cope with to get Daisy's bribery treat before school was over.

I have said it before and I will no doubt say it again; I love driving my car at the moment. I know. Sorry, but I do. It was the best drive I think I've ever had!

I sang all the way there and all the way back and wanted to go out and do it all over again. A bit speedy but good. I have already had 1 speeding fine cancelled by the police on account of me not being able to make the speed awareness course because of treatment, that was very nice of the Warwickshire Police, but I am sure they wont do it again! So car driven, treat   bought, Starbucks visited and home. Fantastic!

And now I am going to get Daisy from school on my own, the first time since last Wednesday, I can't wait!   So its fair to say, I tested the outside world water, it's not so rock and roll, but I liked it!

p.s. Brazilian wax deal was done!

29th June 2013

So, yesterday was great. Just great. After my trip out I picked Daisy up from school and just had the best time with her, no illness, just me and Daisy - so all was good. But today, even though we had our Saturday magic going on, I have woken up cross and sad with the world and stuff in it. Sometimes I just don't get it and I find people very challenging at times.

Today I have vowed to stop trying to understand those that maybe I never will, lets see how that works out for   me! Problem with me is I feel the need to understand everything

and tend to judge things by my own standards. Isn't it right that I am always right! I have added this to my list of things to conquer whilst having chemo.

Things to conquer whilst having chemo has   been something I have thought a lot of about, the first and foremost being time. How to strike the balance of getting through this treatment, the whole 18 weeks of it, keeping sane and well balanced whilst dealing with what having cancer and chemo does to your head, not just your   body. It's a little bit of a mind f**k at times to be honest. And when in this frame of mind, I struggle to understand things that are happening around me. So maybe I just won't and be done with it! When I think about the last treatment, that's October, too far away! Then the surgery comes after, today I'm not happy about any of it and am struggling to find my good attitude towards it. Its taken a leave of absence.

Today everything is making me sad as this is just rubbish at times and I guess this is one of those times. Seems I have misplaced my boxing gloves, or someone is hiding them, either way they are no where in sight.

So a picnic beckons at Attingham Park now, looking forward to walking in the fresh air and sunshine, lets hope   I don't punch anyone who walks in my path!   I have forced myself to walk most days, I believe it is good for my recovering soul. Lets' hope that works today.

p.s. On the plus side I did have a good dream! I was dancing and was being twirled around a dance floor without a care in the world. Fantastic! This is when I want real life and the dream word to collide, sometime soon would be good.

PPS. I'll apologise now for a not so happy post, but the reason I'm writing this is to remember, so there you go!

30th June 2013

We all have bad days. Most people don't write about it on a blog that's all! But I am as this is about the good, the bad and the ugliness of all this nonsense and just to show to myself that I can't be the annoyingly upbeat person I am most of the time. So, tried as I might to get my head back on the right way around again yesterday, it was a struggle. Even Plan B didn't work.

By Plan B I of course mean THE PlanB, mine and Nessa's shared boyfriend! I could even see a little bit of a 'oh no not Plan B again mummy' look on Daisy's face when I put it on, the 1 track I can actually put on in front of her that is.

All my 'go to' things to lift my mood were just laughing in my face and making fun of me. Attingham Park brought what it always does; walking, playing,   laughing, sunshine and good company, just yesterday it was with a heavy heart.

A minor miracle did however happen. I went out on my own for a bit and when I came home Daisy had painted me the most amazing picture of a rainbow, I won't bore you too much about it as I do know that other people's kid's drawings are only of interest to their own parents, but it did the job for me! Daisy has a very special 'in tune' button to her mummy that actually makes my heart melt at times. So, I went in search for my boxing gloves and found them lurking in my deepest darkest moments and whipped them back into boxing shape again.

There is sometimes a bit of a 'f**k it' moment in all this when you just have to say to yourself 'it'll be good in the end'! If I say that over and over enough times it sometimes pulls me out of myself and back on the annoyingly upbeat train I'm on most of the time. You'll also be please to know I didn't punch anyone in the park yesterday however tempting it was at times! (I would never!).

What a difference a day makes, bright and breezy, full of all things good with the world and back on that train, sitting in first class with my eye on the prize, getting to the end of this particular journey in one piece.

So today I plan on reading. I've not read anything for ages due to severe lack of concentration, so I am excited that I now think I can, bring it on Russell Brand! Oh and of course paint my toe nails, very important.

1st July 2013

Just as I was getting out the Die Hard trilogy to watch, Nessa (sister) packed her bags and decided to fly my nest, can't think why! She has gone back to sunny Cornwall and left me to my own devices for the next 10 days! She has been the best and has got me back to being me again, ready for it all to start again next week. But I do have 10 days of being me before the chemo kicks back into gear.

So, today I had to go to the Shrewsbury cancer   unit. I haven't been there since   my radiotherapy finished which feels like such a long time ago, but actually it was only 4 weeks. More on that in a minute, but first I have to say that as I sat there waiting I was amongst other people with cancer, the name of the unit kind of gives that away, but this time I felt more like I fit   in. Crazy. Throughout my whole radiotherapy I felt like a fish out of water, but it seems I have earned my cancer stripes with it being my second time.

Such a busy 4 weeks -surgery x 2, diagnosis, CT scan, results and first cycle of chemo nearly done, and of course decorating.

My poor paint brushes have been severely neglected recently, they had a little outing last night when I managed some stealth painting before my sister caught me out.

Una from the Saturdays has just been to see me for my toxicity check up. She is convinced my hair isn't going anywhere. She described the feeling that people get when its falling out and I am very pleased to say that I am not having any of them, so let's hope Mr. Blinky Eyes wasn't right on that particular point. She also made me feel better about the lack of concentration stuff that's going on. It's called chemo brain. Apparently it gets better after the 3rd treatment and stays good after, lets see shall we.

So I got the thumbs up from Una today and off she went on her way safe in the knowledge that she was going to be back next week to do it to me all over again. So bring on my new lease of life for the next 10 days anyway and let's see what rock and roll the world brings me.

2nd July 2013

Safe in the knowledge that I have a bone-fide condition called chemo brain, I have relaxed a little into the 'not being able to hold my focus on very much for very long' ness that is currently part of me and feel positively giddy at the prospect of the glorious 8 days stretching out in front of me! Usually those

8 days would have filled me with utter dread and when I say usually I mean since having cancer, as 8 days of time with nothing 'planned' would mean I would have to think about what was actually happening to me.

I became very good at distracting myself, in fact I was the master of distraction just to make sure I wasn't ever left with my own very scary thoughts. You know, constantly being with other people, obsessing over anything other than cancer, with detrimental consequences I might add and even sleeping with the TV on to drown the cancer demons from my head.

What a difference a second diagnosis makes. I say   that flippantly, I don't mean it that way as its been   the hardest thing I've ever had to do, but I wonder if it saved me from myself in a very bizarre way or am I just making the best of a bad job! Nothing a good therapist couldn't have sorted out I guess. But as it stands, I did have to do it a second time and now I am doing it very differently. PHEW!

No obsessing about anything other than the colour of my walls at home, lots of time on my own which has been ok in fact I'm quite good company it seems and the TV is well and truly off at sleepy time. I also am not waiting for any results which has normally been the case so knowing I am going to be more than OK and currently well enough to do stuff that takes   no thinking or focus and not much energy then I'm all good even though I am describing myself as an old lady, not the spritely 33-year-old I really am!

So, 8 glorious days. Una from the Saturdays was trying to persuade me to do some gardening, I might. I was telling her about my mad decorating frenzies, she approved. It seems s

he's a little bit of a natural healing type of person as well as a chemo nurse, now you couldn't get more contradictory really! But she approved of my current methods of distraction as opposed to my previous methods, in fact when she's here it's as if she's looking into my soul. She also approved of watching James Bond whilst having chemo. Phew!

I dare say I may have a few re decorated rooms by the end of the 8 days but that will be down to lack of sleeping, not avoidance tactics. Two things actually, I don't have a vast mansion to keep doing so much painting, far from it and I am following doctor's orders to the letter.

It was suggested earlier by my lovely boss that I was being a bit of a maverick about my meds, no, no, no! I will take everything given to me to get through all this, I'm not one to pass up doctor's orders. It was a joy to talk about someone else yesterday, or should I say for someone else to talk about something else, mainly themselves, seems I can always count on James to display his caring side!

So in my very giddy household last night, Daisy went to bed in her bikini, perfect attire for a Monday night don't you think, and I carried on feeling positively excited that I may have just moved a little step further on this journey, in my posh first class cabin that I've managed to keep hold of, into accepting what is happening to me. I also had to accept that the new Die Hard film was not up to scratch and that's putting it mildly, very disappointing but I am sure that my sister was glad she didn't have to sit through it with me!   Bring on day 1 of my 8 days of glorious rock and roll....

3rd July 2013

So day 1 of my glorious 8 was, well fairly glorious, in my own chemo fuelled way. To anyone else it would probably come across as quite dull. To me, pre January 2nd or mid cancer breakdown, it would have been very dull. It's quite amazing what can make you happy when you actually stop and think about it, when not flying around at the speed of light or when not on that juggernaut to cancer breakdownsville. I'm so glad I swapped that juggernaut for this first class cabin I'm currently managing to keep myself in.

I do like good eyebrows! My Oncologist can vouch for the fact that I ask him every time I see him about the likelihood of me losing my eyebrows.

I can see people looking at me a little odd when I declare my distress at losing them, you know not as much as the debilitating tiredness, nausea and all the other joyful side effects this causes, but my eyebrows! Una from the Saturdays

is with me on this however, in fact she's with me on the whole hair must stay on my head process that I'm going through, so again she approves.

So yesterday I decided to look on the positive side of this treatment and I went to get my eyebrows threaded. I can't tell you how excited I was at this (see, dull) There is just something very good about good eyebrows and I wanted my good eyebrows back. I had to ask them not to mess with my hair as they always do, no idea why but they do, but to focus all their eyebrow magic only at my eyebrows. I got there all on my own, had the best wander around the posh shops and then the magic happened! I then took myself off for a coffee and sat and people watched for ages whilst laughing to myself that I had in fact planned my day around some eyebrows that may not be with me in a matter of days.

The horrible hair loss stuff starts around week 3, as of tomorrow I am in week 3. Let's see what happens. Mr. Blinky eyes swears I'll keep my eyebrows but will lose the hair on my head. Una from the Saturdays swears I will keep the hair on my head only based on what she sees daily and

the effects the cold cap has on others with the same dose of chemo as me. In the end, what happens will just happen and no doubt I will either learn to make it look as if I have eyebrows or I'll learn to have no hair for a short time, either way, its temporary and I'll move through it, as I am with all of this.

I then decided that I needed some permanent sunshine in my house and went to get some special sunshine yellow paint mixed up so I can paint the front door a sunny yellow. That way I have my very own happy sunshine to welcome us home. I did try and explain this to my ex, he just told me I had incredibly bad taste. Well, maybe, but just not in decorating. So paint bought, the man in the paint shop approved of my yellow paint, in fact I think he even said that was a very good idea, ha, bad taste my ass! I got home and decided to rip out a whole part of my garden. I really need to plan these things a bit better! I get these ideas, usually whilst doing something completely different, on this occasion having eyebrow magic. I had this amazing idea that this particular bit of garden isn't right and if I did something quite drastic then it would be great! I believe I am quite possibly right.

I then sat down after my trip out, eyebrow magic, people watching, paint mixing and brick ripping up and was very pleased that I've had good company all day.

My own. Without a cancer demon in sight, in fact I welcomed my little pesky cancer demons in and gave them a big cuddle, that got them! I was also very pleased as this time last week I hadn't left the house for over a week, I've really got to make the most of these good weeks it seems, which of course I intend to!

I then promptly fell asleep.

Day 2 of my glorious 8 and Nessa (BF) is winging her way down as we speak and whatever we do it will be filled with our very own glorious rock and roll...

4th July 2013

So day 3 of my glorious 8 was full of Nessa gloriousness, with her new found love of all things Brazilian. I'm so glad. Along with our mutual appreciation of eyebrows and a very good mascara, it's fair to say I'm a bit of an expert on mascara and so hope I keep hold of my lovely lashes. We went out for lunch which was ace and then back home, for a fairly low key but funny as afternoon. We watched a Ted talks by Brene Brown, highly recommend it, as it really resonated with us both. Nessa said it reminded her of me, if you watch it you will see exactly why! I do believe we have a little in common about how we come across. We then watched the only type of film I think I can follow currently due to the chemo brain thing, Bridesmaids. Funny, funny, funny, a little annoying at times but very funny.

I love these visits. I think we both forget why we are doing it sometimes and I know we both get that heart lurching feeling when we both remember. The little chemo demons creep in every now and again to remind me it's going to be starting again very soon. I KNOW I want to scream at them, but I can manage not to scream out loud like some mad person

and get on with having some good times out of this. Who would have thought that was possible, certainly not me a few weeks ago I tell you! When this is all over I swear I will come home to Nessa every now and again just pottering around my house making me eat marmite and fresh fruit, I hope I do anyway! Or we will be too busy fulfilling all the items on my list of things I am going to do when all this over that is growing by the day.

So I woke up underneath my amazing rainbow that Daisy made that now has a permanent place over my bed, always holding out for that pot of gold it seems, well now it's there right above me! Ness and I drank coffee and watched crap day time TV whilst trying to muster up the motivation to do some boring official stuff. There is so much paper work involved with having cancer. If anyone ever had any ideas that you got cancer and just spent all the time being ill and freaked out, let me tell you that's so wrong.

Or maybe other people do it for others I don't know but I get that joy all by myself!

Paperwork is not my strong point but I'm getting quite the organised one since this has happened. Then the lovely Nessa had to leave to get back into the real world.

As Nessa was driving up to Leeds, Lindsay, my oldest pal, was driving from Leeds to me. When I say oldest I don't

mean in age, she's not a doddering old lady, quite the opposite, she's a gorgeous spritely same age as me girl!

Lindsay and I have known each other since we were 4 and lived across the street from each other up until we were about 16 and have known each other nearly all our lives. Lindsay also has had the same misfortune as me of having breast cancer twice. Crazy, in fact when I was first diagnosed in January a lot of people who had experienced breast cancer for themselves tried to contact me to try and help me which was lovely, but I couldn't speak to any of them as it scared me too much as everyone's story is different. Lindsay is the only person to have had breast cancer that I wanted to speak to. I remember driving up to Leeds to see her to ask her loads of questions and I remember being really scared. But in true Lindsay style, she very matter of factly told me what she thought I needed to know and nothing more which is exactly what I needed.

Today I asked question after question about side effects and what does this mean if this happens etc. and we just sat in disbelief at times that this was and had happened to both of us. Much discussion about if

I'm going to lose my eyebrows or not, see another girl after my own heart! And then we just concluded that what ever happens will just happen and I'll deal with it when and if it

does. But she did remember that there were no sensations in her head pre hair loss which bodes well and her cold cap worked enough the first time around not to get the wigs out.

We both were struggling however with the something good out of this though, but both convinced there is something. I can't wait to find out what! But it was truly lovely to sit and chat like we'd never been apart really. And then something happened. I think I have started having hay fever again! Now it's not normal to be happy about this, as it was pointed out to me earlier. There is a theory that says some people stop having hay fever when they have cancer. But   please don't assume this is the case for everyone. But, last year I didn't have hay fever and I normally get it every year and last year I had cancer but just didn't know it. So I'm happy as my body is getting back to the no cancer status I want it to and if that means having hay fever then bring it on!

And then a knock on the door and a lovely hamper arrives from James (boss James). Very nice James, thank you! I have put the champagne on ice ready for when I have   some celebrating to do.

Daisy of course opened the hamper and as I was reading it all out to her she looked at me and said 'it's really nice mummy that your boss has sent this, it really shows he cares and its nice to care for people' BLESS HER!

So its fair to say my day 3 of my glorious 8 was truly glorious. I love it when people surprise me and I love it when I get ace visitors. A bit more rock and roll and I sure do like it!

5th July 2013

Just as I finished yesterdays update and posted it, I had a flick through what else in the world was going on and saw that Bernie Nolan had died of breast cancer. I have to say it literally stopped me in my tracks. I am not one to usually be so effected by other peoples, those I don't know, very sad news, but this, at this time of my life, effected me hugely. I could not stop thinking about it. I had to use all the logic I had last night to talk myself out of a fall. I saw pictures of her whilst she was having her chemo and saw she had no eyebrows, I now know that means she had a different chemo to me and it probably meant her lymph nodes were   effected. Mine were not.

Logic no. 1, my cancer did not spread through my lymph nodes meaning it hasn't got anywhere else in my body from these 2   bloody horrible tumours. And I know a lot of people where it has effected them that are absolutely fine now and have been for years.

My scans were all clear. Logic no. 2. I've had every scan going and nothing was found.

Logic no. 3. I'm having chemo to prevent it coming back, not to kill something that's there now.

Logic no. 4. I'm having a double mastectomy and reconstruction in November (ish) to minimise the chances of it recurring in the place that clearly I'm vulnerable.

Ok. Pep talk over and back on my feet with those boxing gloves firmly in place.

And Breath. Again.

So, I'm on day 4 of my glorious 8 but today I have those horrible butterflies back. I feel nervous, as if I'm waiting for something to happen or for someone to tell me some bad news. Surely bad news can bugger of for a while for me, haven't I had enough of that recently. It would be good if the world was nice to me for a while as I'm sure I'm nice to the world, isn't that how it works! Put in what you want to get back, treat others how you would want to be treated yourself, smile and the world smiles with you and all the other clichéd phrases we all know and love. Or am I so used to having bad news this year that it's a self fulfilling prophecy. I feel a little vulnerable to the elements today, to those forces I feel I have no control over.

I have been quite good so far at trying to take some control over a disease that can only be described as evil.

Whether what I have done makes any difference, who knows,but psychologically it has and I'm sure that sometimes means more. I've practically cut out diary from my diet as its been proven to reduce the risks of breast cancer, I juice so many vegetables every day that if I'm not getting my full intake of vitamins and minerals then I don't actually know how to! I have all the right supplements to help me get through chemo and to help me stay strong, I'm not drinking any alcohol through this treatment and I'm trying my best to walk everyday even though I don't always want to as I'm sure it helps. But today, even though I should be able to fly like superwoman with all that, the reality sometime hits that its just a bloody horrible disease, one that killed both my parents and has effected so many people I know. I am very determined for this not to do the same to me.

So, on that not so happy note (sorry), I am going out for a walk in the park with the lovely Christine and am going to have one of my lovely treats. I love treats, like we all do, and my treats come in many different shapes and sizes, todays comes in the shape of a Starbucks coffee! The most un rock and roll thing going, I know, but in the first week of chemo I couldn't stand the smell off coffee and therefore didn't have any. So now I can and will make the most of my ability to drink my favourite non alcoholic drink! I'll save my favourite alcoholic drink, mojitos, for when I'm better and out of   this nonsense. Now that is something I am very much looking forward to!

ps. I've still got hay fever! Yeah!

<u>6th July 2013</u>

Crashed and burned. That's the only way I can describe   what happened
to me yesterday! I'm fine now, in fact I'm more than fine but yesterday it
all went a bit wrong! I did have a brief interlude from my crashing and
burning when I basked in Christine's warm happy glow which was very
lovely, but when I was left to my own devices those pesky cancer demons
came at me in full force, tormenting me like you would not
believe.   So if I was to revert to type, I would have sung 'la la la la la la
la' at the top of my voice with my hands over my ears whilst making
frantic plans to see someone NOW! I would not have let those little
buggers into my head or even entertained the idea I had to maybe deal
with all this nonsense, surely it can be put away in a dark place in my
head to come back and bite me sometime in the near future, just
not   now. Mmm, reminiscent of cancer no. 1's   behaviour!

I didn't do any of that. I let it all happen in my head, oh boy! There was a
hard core rave going on in there last night, not of the nice kind, if in fact
any hard core rave could be nice. I managed to wrestle the pesky demons
and throw logic at them. I actually realised I have logic, more than I ever
realised and boy did it come in handy!

I used to have to borrow logic from others to get me through stuff, or so I
thought. Seems I have my own in abundance.   So I got rid of those
particular demons last night to live another day. Well, to live a lot more
days actually, that's sort of the point. Everywhere I looked yesterday there
was something about cancer, it was as if it was following me around! But
it just goes to show that it's out there. A lot. And for every sad story there
a million happy ones, mines a happy one, that's what I decided last night.

I have various things I say over and over to myself when I need to get myself out of these pickles, things like 'I'll be good' over and over, 'it's not there any more remember!' over and over, I now have a new one. 'Mine's a happy story'. Over and over. Worked a treat last nigh.   Add to the hard core rave going on in my head, a very tired Daisy and we had a right laugh. NOT! Daisy decided to join in the rave in my head and she put on a singing show in the garden for me. Of course this was lovely, in a sort of out of tune way. By the end of it my head was absolutely pounding so I went to bed with Daisy and think I may have even gone to sleep before her.

Day 5 of my glorious 8, I have 4 days left before the treatment kicks in and the sun is shining and everything seems right with the world again.

I feel very happy with my self actually; I think I should get a well done badge or a gold star or something for putting to rest those demons of mine! All on my own as well. My butterflies have also gone, so if I do get bad news at least I'm not waiting for it today. I certainly hope I don't though, no more please!   Today Daisy and I had our Saturday morning in bed together, all good! We have plans a plenty today involving paddling pools and general frolicking in the sun.   Let's see what rock and roll this weekend brings...

8th July 2013

Never underestimate the magic of friendship. Today I am declaring that I am one lucky girl when it comes to my friends. Andy Murray this morning on the news took the words right out of my mouth when he said that it's the people he has surrounded himself with who have got him through all the hard knocks in his career to ultimately winning Wimbledon. I can certainly say that it's the people I am surrounded by who are getting me through the hardest knock I've ever had to face. I can't play tennis. But I am going to get through all this because of those around me.

The 'Nessa's' driving half way across the country practically on a weekly basis to be with me. WOW! Those near, not so near and those across the other side of the world who let me bask in their very warm happy glow and

yesterday, any misguided feelings of not being good enough were soon put right away with the best night out with gin Jayne and the lovely Catriona, who makes a damn good lemon drizzle cake by the way! We were transported to a different land when we sat outside all night having dinner, we could have been anywhere and in fact I could pretend all was normal in the world and that I wasn't in fact getting nervous about chemo again in 3 days. Perfect.

So my headache has come back with a vengeance and I have now realised what it is. Chemo brings about all sorts of side effects that are commonly known and some that are not. The one that most people don't know is that brings about a false state of the menopause. I've not been ready to talk about this to be honest as it also means I am probably infertile now but I think I am getting my head around it. It's better than the alternative of having cancer don't you thin. I may or may not come out of this menopause when the treatment ends, whatever happens I will go through it again when it would be my natural time to do it, at least I will know what to expect and how to deal with it though. But either way I have done in 9 days what it normally takes years to do.

As you would expect I am tackling this in my usual way and am taking all sorts of supplements and reviewing my diet to make sure it doesn't effect me too badly, so far the only thing I can't get rid of are these headaches, so not bad really. The first time around when I had to decide if

I was going to have chemo, I knew that having chemo would make me infertile. I have Daisy and I am no spring chicken – I am lucky there – but it still feels strange knowing that side of my life has gone. My body has changed irreversibly.

It seems painting gets rid of my headache so that's what I intend to do a bit of today to see if it works! Last night we realised why I like painting so much. I am the sort of person that likes to see results. So I go all out to get things done, at work and at home, to get results quite quickly. At the moment everything I am doing is taking time. 18 weeks of chemo then waiting for the surgery which will be done in 2 stages as radiotherapy skin can't be operated on for a year so I will have mismatched boobs for a while! That's fine as they will be amazing by the time I'm done! (something good out   of something bad perhaps! HA!)

But that means more waiting so this whole illness will have taken over more than a year of my life when I am fixed and back to the cancer free land I long to be in. So I think to take some control back I am doing things that I can see some results. And I still can't concentrate enough to read or watch films that are any good, or do much that involves my brain, remember the chemo brain thing, I'm not making it up.

So the sun is shining, I'm a very lucky girl and I'm off to paint something, not rock and roll at all but it works for me today.

9th July 2013

So today started by being a little nervous about what's coming on Thursday. Even though I know what to expect I am still nervous about the whole being ill thing all over again. I have sort of forgotten how it felt. A bit like child birth, well nothing like it really, but only like it as you forget how painful it was. If you remembered there is no way anyone would have more than one child. Also nervous due to the torture that is the cold cap, 4 and half hours of brain freeze to come, but in the name of keeping my hair I will endure what can only be described as bloody awful.

On the whole hair loss thing. My hair is falling out at a rate that I am really not happy with. I have hit the 3-week marker of when it starts to happen, and like clockwork, it's happening. I do have a lot of hair and I was told that my hair would thin out a bit so I should be expecting this. I can tell you there is nothing nice about seeing your hair come out in your hand every time you touch it, more and more as the day has gone on. Even James today tried to prove it was normal by pulling some of his own hair out in the quest to make me feel better, I am sure. It did for a while but there is nothing normal about the amount that is coming out now. What will be will be and I know it's not permanent but it still makes me really sad. And what will be will happen over the next week or so. I guess it's all pat of the cancer deal.

So, I had a great day today. Apart from getting nervous and the hair falling out stuff. I met James (boss) for lunch.

It was very, very nice to talk about lots of things that had nothing to do with cancer or chemo and to talk about work. Oh boy I have missed work! I bet anyone reading this will be saying 'eh!' But I love my job and I can't believe I can't do it at the moment. It was also lovely to see James. Reason no. 2 for being a lucky girl, I work for great people. And I'm not saying that to inflate Mr. Boss's ego as I'm not sure that's possible! The only sad thing about it was on the way home realising it's going to be months before I can go back. Bugger.

Anyway, my plan for tomorrow. I've got a new foot stool coming for my sofa! It seemed really important to me when I was in the 1st week of chemo to get a foot stool and it was really annoying me that my sofa seemed really uncomfortable to me when all I wanted to do was lie on it for days. So as soon as I could muster up the brain power to go online and find the place where the sofa came from, I ordered one and it's winging its way to me as we speak. I also threw in some new covers in the most inappropriate colour going but I don't care. I liked it.

I'm having my blood tested to make sure my white blood cells are ok to have treatment on Thursday, fingers crossed. I'm going shopping for all the things I wanted last time, lets hope I want the same things this time, and Nessa sister will be driving up from Cornwall with 2 very special guinea pigs for Miss Daisy.

Miss Daisy is also Miss superstar Daisy. Had her first school report yesterday and to say she has gone through her parents splitting up, her Dad disappearing for a few weeks and then her mum having cancer twice, lots of surgery and rubbish treatments, she's come out all guns a blazing! That's my girl! So guinea pigs are a very welcome addition to our family, Lucy and Amelia they are called!

Nessa is coming to look after me in my hours of need over the coming days and to watch really crap TV with no volume (sorry!). I can't wait until we get together to do good stuff that doesn't involve chemo drugs, cold caps, meds, frantic washing of hands, hair falling out and crap TV.

So possibly no rock and roll on the horizon for me this week but at least my glorious 8 days have been, well, glorious!   ps. It's my mum's birthday today, even though she's been gone for well over half my life time I still have a little birthday celebration for her. That means cake. I think I'd be pushing it with the sparkly stuff.

10th July 2013

So I cried myself to sleep last night. I can't believe I'm saying that as it's not something you normally admit to really but in

the spirit of remembering why I am writing this then it is something I need to do. I cried myself to sleep for 3 reasons.

The first being; chemo tomorrow and it hitting me like a sledgehammer that this is happening to me. You would have thought I'd got used to the idea by now really,   but sometimes it's like I was told yesterday.

The second because of my hair! Very vain I know, but at the moment I can lose myself in any crowded place and be out in the   open without anyone giving me a second glance and I can pretend all is fine, if my hair goes it becomes   something different and it's the first visual sign of my being ill.

The third, I really wanted someone to hold me tight and tell me it was all going to be good.

Anyway, I decided at some crazy hour of the night/early morning that it really shouldn't matter what's going on with my hair. As Nessa said as long as it means I'm better then so be it. So there we go. I also remembered that I've been super cool about doing this without a soul matey type person and to get over myself. Not sure it's that easy sometimes, but it needs to be.

So, with very little sleep I got Daisy to school and then promptly burst into tears the minute gin Jayne said hello to me. Typical. I cried all the way home whilst my hair was

falling out at an unbelievable rate. I have believed my own hype of keeping my hair. I still might but if it carries on doing what it is today then that looks very doubtful! I haven't prepared myself for losing it.

I know that Its better to have no hair than to have cancer, in fact I know all of this logic. Quite frankly logic can go and take a running jump when it comes to this. I can nearly always find the humour and logic in any situation. I can make the most serious of people laugh in the most inappropriate situations, my surgeon, my oncologist, my friends and family when they have been in pieces about me. I have logically talked myself around from all sorts of dark places and successfully brought myself out of juggernaut hell, but I have nothing when it comes to my hair. I just can't explain how it makes me feel, apart from I want to hide away and not come out until its grown back. That's no good as I'll end up on that   same juggernaut I was a few weeks ago heading to breakdownsville and I'm not going back there, ever.

In an attempt to get over myself I had a lovely hour with Helen, we drank tea and ate ginger biscuits on   the veranda, very lovely. And I went to get some cotton PJ's ready for my few days not being able to move much and my foot stool and

new sofa covers arrived. I have to say I am very pleased with those.

My blood has been taken, fingers crossed I'm ready for round 2, however much I don't want to have it, it will piss me off even more if I can't have it on time.

On the plus side the nurse said that the amount of hair in my hand that I had just come out of my head was not a lot. She said it normally comes out in clumps, mine is not.

Yet. Maybe I should just stop running my hands through it! Get over yourself ALEX! So now time for the big clean and tidy and general getting ready for my imminent fate. I may even squeeze in a bit of painting... rock and roll heaven!

11th July 2013

So, it's here. Cycle no. 2. My blood was all good and I'm ready for a 2pm chemo and cold cap session. Apparently. Last night my paint brushes had a treat as I couldn't sleep so a little bit of moonlight painting was done. My late night activities sure aren't what they used to be. The only problem was that in the name of being creative I had mixed my own paint. It ran out before the job had been done. Not good. So this morning I am looking at a very random wall that should have been calm and serene and super stylish. It is in fact stripy and silly and completely unfinished! BUT it could almost be that I have done this on purpose as it gives me the perfect distraction this morning to finish it before 2pm arrives. Time may in fact go at a snail pace today so I have my perfect past time to keep me company. Nessa (sister) has driven through the night to get here, so she can sleep before dreaded treatment whilst I paint, works all round.

So yesterday my footstool and covers arrived. Very exciting. Yes, I know I need to get out more, but I   was genuinely excited, that was until I realised how hard it was to change it all. It took me nearly all day but my word, the results were mighty impressive, even though I do say so myself. Of course this busy 'ness was all in the name of getting over myself as yesterday was a bit of a tricky day. I have them, as we all do, I just write about mine. But today is another day and I feel ready to take on what's coming again, I may retract that statement as the day goes on, but right now I'm feeling better about the treatment today and I'm even feeling better about my hair. That of course may have something to do with Nessa being here too. I read up again about what happens through treatment and the cold cap at some unearthly hour and actually what's happening is normal. Well, as normal as it ever will be. I reserve the right to feel wobbly about this particular subject until I have a full head of hair again.

I tried really hard to find a little bit of humour in the whole hair thing. I'm good a humour in situations, it helps me get my head around them and through the other side. I almost had something about convertible cars and wind in your hair but decided it wasn't that funny.

Mainly as I don't have a convertible car, Mr. Boss Man wouldn't let me have one this time around, something to do with family car to convertible may equal a mid

life crisis with a bit of cancer thrown in   the mix. Good point and the fact I'm not actually a fan of convertible cars, unless of course it was an Aston Martin. Not sure they are on the company car list though!

So, I have my fennel and cotton PJ's at the ready   and nearly everything sorted to be out of action for a few days. I'm going to have a Starbucks treat this morning before I can't stand the smell of coffee again and I'm going to eat, drive my car, let my sister sleep and paint before the time comes to get those boxing gloves on again. They are in sight, waiting and ready. Phew! I've also got James Bond to keep me company through the treatment, Of course! Here goes. See you on the other side of me being a third of the way through. Yeah!

Ps. Guinea pigs, Amelia and Lucy have arrived. What have I

done! I really can't keep getting animals to distract Daisy from my illness and treatment. I'll have a small zoo before long.

Pps. Miss Daisy hasn't even noticed my badly painted wall this morning! My creative home decorating skills (I say that loosely) are clearly lost on her.

12th July 2013

So, chemo no. 2 done! Floating around my system as we speak causing its usual havoc. I can't remember feeling quite this bad last time, but Nessa (sister) swears I did. I haven't got my self out of bed since it all kicked in at around 7pm last night.

I had a different nurse yesterday. Una from the Saturdays is sunning herself in Majorca so I had Gerry. Now affectionally known as Gerry from The Spice Girls! So Gerry from The Spice girls was as lovely, as you can imagine. She was also very informative on the old hair loss thing that's happening which made me feel better. It seems I'm on a super high dose of the red drug that makes up the FEC'ing stuff and that's the one causing the hair loss, amongst all the other side effects I'm getting the most of. It turns out that I'm sensitive, possibly more than some, to this red one. Well, I would be wouldn't I, nothing straight forward about me it seems. As we are all individual and some people can have the same dose as me and not have the same effect as me. Always knew I was a sensitive soul. She also said that people with my type of cancer have this high dose as its been proven to increase the likelihood of it not coming back. That little bit of knowledge = me feeling better about the whole hair loss thing. Simple.

So my hair has definitely been invited to a much better party than the one my body can provide right now as it's having a mass exodus, not necessarily on my head as no one really could tell the difference yet, its just when

I touch it, or walk in the wind as I did yesterday and couldn't work out what was falling on my face. That'll be my hair then, queue me crying all around Tesco's, not a good look. It's like someone came and gave me a full body wax in the night and I've woken up with significantly less hair than I went to bed with. That doesn't both me at all, in fact its quite nice. Its just the stuff on my head that freaks me out. It's so distressing to see it come out. In a couple of weeks, I will know what it's doing and then will be able to make that scary call of giving my self a no.1 with the clippers. Arrgg!

I'm back to not wanting any noise or TV or music or reading magazines or wanting to eat anything although I have just forced scrambled eggs down me. I am missing Daisy's first spots day which is on now which I am absolutely gutted about and I am now going back to sleep, sad about the sports day but very relieved I am now 1 third of the way through this scary nonsense that is chemo. Oh and Nessa, whilst showing Gerry from The Spice girls out yesterday called her chemo spice! And I think told her she had to wear a union jack dress next time she came, will we see her again I wonder.   So my rock and roll today will mostly involve sleeping,   that works for me!

13th July 2013

So, I made it through yesterday. Boy,

that was quite tough! I am so sure I wasn't that bad last time, but no amount of trying to convince Nessa (sister) that this was worse was working! She is sure I was as bad. Just goes to show what you can forget. Anyway, I made it and today I think I am better than I was last time! I slept loads yesterday, in between feeling unbelievably sick, but I mainly slept. This morning I have been awake since 5.30am and have been up and even made a cup of tea, and drank it. Now I know that seems very, very simple and I agree it does. But trust me, there was no way I was doing that yesterday. These blooming

waves of nausea just hit me, that's one problem, but I've just had all my meds, as instructed so let's hope I stay awake for more of the day today, and if I don't, I don't as I know tomorrow will be loads better if last time is anything to go by.

My sense of smell isn't as sensitive as last time and I am currently watching the TV at a more respectable volume so maybe I am getting the hang of this a bit more, who knows, as long as I get through, I don't care.

I have my eye on the prize of round 6 on or about the 3rd October, that's all that matters.

So Daisy got through sports day in the heat and came back here to say hi to me, or so I thought. She in fact came running in, I heard Nessa say

I was in bed, she just carried on outside and went straight to Lucy and Amelia, her 2 new friendly Guinea Pigs, typical!! I actually had to come downstairs to see her. I so take 2nd place, for now anyway. All good though as she was over the moon with them and very, very happy. She also got smiley face of the week at school. The prize is to organise all the registers next week, that may sound horrible to some but to Daisy it means she can be bossy and organised and be in charge. Now I wonder where she's got that from. That's my girl, again.

So, today I will do what ever my body tells me to, lets see. It will be nothing exciting and definitely nothing rock and roll!

ps. Have you noticed I have not mentioned my hair! I didn't touch it all day yesterday, I was a bit scared to! What a woos!

4th July 2013

Check me out. I am doing better than last time. Apart from day's 1 and 2, I think it's a given they will always be a bit rubbish, yesterday was much better than last time and today so far has also been better. I know that as I have been awake since 2.30am, not great really but not feeling that bad whilst being awake is the good bit!

Clearly I had gone to bed at 7pm so I had in effect had a whole night's sleep! So yesterday I managed to stay awake from 5.30am to 7pm with only a 2-hour sleep in the middle. Last cycle I was asleep for this whole day. I made my own breakfast, scrambled eggs, and pretty much was OK. I didn't move much, but who needs to when its 30 degrees outside and you've just had chemo! The only issue was waking up when possibly some people reading this were just going to   bed. Jealous? Me? Very!

So I am feeling rather pleased with myself. And long may it continue. I have even watched the news and other more exciting programmes again today, which was not an option last time, not sure why. I still have to turn over anything cancer related though. I even had to turn off Sex and The

City yesterday as Samantha got breast cancer, no no no no no not for my viewing right now, if ever to be honest. But this cycle feels better, maybe as Daisy is away having a ball and letting me sleep and not worry about her and maybe I'm just getting used to it a bit, how is that possible? Lindsay it seems you were right, how could I have not believed you!

My sister however was missing in action as she got terribly lost in Shrewsbury. I'm still not sure how that happened, something to do with being on a big fennel mission and no one selling it. She ended up coming home with a guinea pig cage.

So, I'm now only on 1 set of meds, from 5 and feeling ok under the circumstances and as long as I don't do much I think I will be just fine. But I guess the not doing too much is the issue really, as it's so not in my nature! A little lesson to learn no doubt.

My plan for the day. Not to do too much. Well, that   already hasn't happened as I was caught painting this morning by Nessa. Well, what else am I to do after being awake for so long with not a lot else going on. It was annoying me unfinished. My biggest challenge is not to get too jealous at my lack of rock and roll when I'm sure everyone else in the world is doing something really rock and roll and exciting out in the sunshine.

<u>15th July 2013</u>

It's a funny thing doing what I am doing at the moment as I'm in a funny little bubble that the outside world doesn't touch too much in these first few days and I think its quite easy to forget why I feel quite as rough as I do and why I feel a little down from time to time. And then I remember. That can go one of two ways really, a bit of relief that there is a valid reason to being in such a strange place and then sometimes just sad. Sad because it feels like time is going to take its time to get me to the end of this mad journey.

My body clock is all over the place too and I am sure what ever you think about in those dark hours before dawn are much more serious than they would be if it was light outside! That's my excuse anyway.

So, my body clock is a little shot due to me wanting to sleep every time I eat. Very random. Maybe also the heat, which I am not complaining about at all as it's lovely to see the sun shining, I haven't been outside remember since Thursday, my house is just perfect for this as I have an outside in bit so it's been working a treat. So I have done that very

Alex Jagger

annoying thing of being awake since 3.30am this time, an hour later than yesterday, woo!

Back to this little bubble of mine that I'm currently in, I'm not sure how I feel about it today really. I'd like it to be a normal Monday morning, you know, going to   work, rushing

around to get out of the house on time driving down the M6 in all the traffic and so on. That sounds so appealing to me right now. Instead I'll be at home, not able to do much. I am sure this gets better and I am sure that by the end of this week I will be back to being able to do more than I am doing now and I know I need to just surrender myself to this week, I'm not sure I will ever get used to this, in fact, I hope I never have to. Just 4 more times and I'm done, remember, 1 third of the way through, in 2 weeks I'll be half way through, almost!

I am trying to bargain with time it seems to see how to get myself through this, not sure how that's possible really but I am giving it a go. If only I could read, watch decent TV, eat without feeling exhausted afterwards, not feel rough, walk around, just do stuff! I know I will. Just not   yet. Bloody frustrating is all this is to be honest today. Oh and it would be nice if my hair would either stop doing what it's doing or just all fall out, this thinning out stuff   is mighty distressing. I am feeling less upset about it now actually as I can't stop what ever is going to happen, and it will, of course, grow back, apparently in quite an amazing way and I have justified it by knowing that by Christmas I will have hair again if it does in fact all fall out.

Knowing me is to know that a decision has to be made as I don't like being in between anything, hair or no hair! I was always told I was very

black or white, very few grey areas

with me. Maybe this is one of those annoying lessons I need to learn.

I am a quick learner. In most cases I   am anyway. This nonsense though
is proving to be a bit of a challenge at times.

Yesterday was mighty tricky in so far as I was feeling as flat as a pancake.
I know I can make even the trickiest of pancakes flip and taste more or
less acceptable

 whatever the circumstances, but yesterday was hard. Luckily Nessa
(sister) was there to pick me up off the floor, or scrape me off the ceiling
which ever way you want to look at it which got me through the day.
Daisy also provided the best distractions and noise and frivolity that was
sorely needed.

So, the learning quickly thing, I think I have to just get my head around
the fact that this is a journey that will take me to all sorts of different
places, happy and sad, frustrating and accepting but ultimately better. So
what ever twists and turns that I find myself on, they all pass and that's
what came out of yesterday as I carried on, did not stop and surrender
myself to feeling flat, I tried really hard to get my self out of that hole.
And I did. Today I feel better. I woke up at a more normal time after a
normal nights sleep and feel a bit more like me again, looking forward to
getting on with some stuff today, rather than dreading what the day will
bring, remember I have my eye on that prize at the end of this.

We had a plan for the day. Nessa was on a mission to get me back to some sort of sanity. We went out, bought gardening supplies and food and paint, I know, sorry! We came home after having a very unhealthy treat that I can't even bring myself to write. Needless to say they were f

abulous and very tasty and I don't care and both Nessa and I are sworn to secrecy! We came home, and did something I have not done before. Gardenin. It was great and we actually made some parts of my garden look really good which helped immensely. Granted some look even worse, temporarily as I did get a little carried away lopping things down, like trees, of the small and dead variety, but that will be sorted today. I had no idea that gardening could be so therapeutic and actually good and rather satisfying.

I have taken Daisy to school. That sounds so normal, but I had to be walked back by Nic, Josh and Ella to make sure I got back as I was super wobbly. How silly. What the mind wants to do and the body can't, just yet anyway. Sanity intact, I am ready to tackle my garden and what ever else the day throws at me.

17th July 2013

It's what dreams are made of! Well, good dreams   anyway. And last night I had the best dreams and the best nights sleep and have woken up ready to fight another million years. The power of the subconscious.

Anyway, yesterday was a much better day, although wiped out from my over active mind over what my body can do scenario and the heat thrown in for good measure, it   was still a good day. Me and Nessa had a bit of groundhog day going on as we more or less repeated our trip out from the day before, including illicit treat again! But all good as we actually got loads done and had a good day. I even made tea for us all which was super tasty, even though I do say so myself!

So now my thoughts have been transported to important matters such as how avoid having a hunch back with amazing new boobs. That's what gets talked about at the school gates these days you know. It does if Nic and I are anything to do with it anyway. So whilst trying to list the positives about my current nonsense, of course the little silver lining that is fully reconstructed boobs by amazing plastic surgeon was highlighted as being, well, a highlight! Forget the reason why I will be spending time with said plastic surgeon, his name is Dan, 'Dan the Boob Man' I affectionately call him, he drives a Porsche with a private reg plate. How do I know that?

Every time I go to hospital there is a car with a private plate with the name Dan and it's a Porsche and he's a plastic surgeon, my math's may not be great but I reckon that adds up to being his. I've also met him so know its his. Anyway, Dan the Boob Man will be sprinkling magic dust in my

direction at some point after treatment is over, along with my friendly surgeon, who has only just started calling me Alex, cautiously I might add, you know in case I inappropriately launch myself at him or something.

So, then conversation moved to diet and the fact I have changed mine quite a lot since all this, one thing being dairy, as in I don't eat very much of it. Gerry from the Spice Girls told me off a little for this as she said it's important for osteoporosis as now I am more susceptible to that after chemo, just another little joy of this. Bizarrely I have also been craving dairy so have given in and have been back on it in full swing as clearly my body needs it right now. A moment of horror came across our faces earlier as the risk of getting a hunch back due to osteoporosis just does   not work with amazing new boobs, how on earth can you show them off if you can't even stand up straight. Not the look I was hoping for. Let's face it, the way my luck has been going recently I really can't risk any hunch back issues. I would be the girl who survived cancer twice but now stoops with an unfortunate hump! And that certainly isn't acceptable when trying to rock the single girl look! No amount of Feng Shui will help that.

18th July 2013

With the hunch back crisis averted and much milk consumed I was l left to my own devices with thoughts of Dan the Boob

Man, Mr. cautious surgeon and all things at the end of   this nonsense. So all good as I travelled the world in my head, solved all the issues I may have ever had,

saved loads of money and changed the world at work which of course is my mission, I even dreamt I said that last night. Is that a sign I need to get out more, when dreaming of work, changing the world and unbelievably PPS hours at one of my old pubs. I wonder!

So, I very impressively got everything on my list done yesterday ready for some true rock and roll with Nessa (BF) today. She came, we went and we conquered. We conquered lunch out, much laughing, me getting my hair cut, who else do you know having chemo with potential hair loss getting a hair cut. A super splendid pedicure and the best chill out room going, more laughing, Daisy entertainment, much more laughing and now home to chill out a bit. Perfect.

19th July 2013

So, she came, we went and we conquered and now she's gone leaving a path of merriment in her wake and leaving me to my wonderful own devices again. Not before realising there was a website called 'parking like a twat', and one that shows inanimate objects that look like faces, you know the important things in life.

Anyway, Una from The Saturdays has been to see me.

I love Una from The Saturdays, not just because she is my very nice nurse but because she gave me the best news today. She is a massive advocate of the cold cap system. She has also been very cautiously honest with me about what to expect with my hair. She came today as my notes from last treatment were that my hair loss was quite rapid, I was freaking out at that time if I remember rightly, so she wanted to see for herself today. When I opened the door to her she looked like she was about to wrap her arms around me with the warmest sigh of relief I've seen. I honestly don't look any different and she told me that by now my hair would have gone, no questions. Bloody amazing! I made her check it and made her tell me a number of times that she was super happy with my progress, and my hair! Yipee for cold caps and yippee for Claire with the big hair and the biggest yippee for Una from The Saturdays.

Una from The Saturdays also comes to check on my emotional status as well as physical and she is very firm with me about keeping me, me. I swear she sees into my soul. I now agree that chemo does get a really bad name, sure it's not pleasant but it kills the big C and it's not actually as scary as everyone makes it out to be as the drugs that control the side effects are amazing. Of course I say that now. I was terrified first time around. So, here's to me being like me again!

So, with the hunch back crisis averted and now potential hair loss crisis currently averted it seems I'm on a roll. Maybe I can rock this whole thing on my terms and in my own way. Bring it on I say!

20th July 2013

All things Australian is where it's at today. My bestest, most favourite Aussie girl is back from her travels and we are hopefully winging her to way to her today and we absolutely cannot wait! Daisy and I are getting a little giddy with excitement it has to be said. That and it's also the holidays for Daisy and some may say for me. Not sure how I feel about that really, not my idea of a holiday to be injected with toxic poison every 3 weeks, have so many meds just to stop me from being sick and to be so vulnerable to infections that I need to run a mile from every snively nose but then again we're all different!

So I got a little carried away yesterday - I know, shocker. Una from the

Saturdays told me before she arrived yesterday that she was taking blood too. That was unusual as it was 2 weeks early so in my most vivid imaginary mind I had it that maybe my cycle was speeding up.

Before she arrived I had, in my head, actually finished my treatment 6 weeks earlier than planned,

had all my surgery, as in my head my skin miraculously recovered on the radiotherapy side quicker mainly due to Dan The Boob Mans magic no doubt and I was back at work, healthy and fighting fit being the Alex Jagger I know and love well before Christmas! In fact, in my head, by Christmas it was all just a distant memory.

So, back in the real world Una from the Saturdays had a good laugh at my plan, it would kill me she said. Then I would be the girl who survived cancer twice, averted hunchback and hair loss crisis but was poisoned in trying to bargain with time debacle.

The blood test was in fact a mistake and none was taken but to compensate from the deflation of my imaginary plan the hair news took me on a whole different journey of wonderment. I was so happy about that news that I found myself telling people I didn't even know about it. They must have wondered what on earth I was on about, why was that blonde girl so happy about keeping her hair! Looking back, it feels like I was skipping through the school playground singing 'I'm going to keep my hair, I'm going to keep my hair, I'm going to keep my hair' and so on, you get the picture! Let's hope I do now after all that! What will be will be, I'm still cool with that based on my luck!

So, it also seems I can actually pass for the 33-year-old my super big boss, who wants to

borrow my cold cap by the   way, thought I was. My skin has   done something quite amazing. It has of course renewed at such a rate due to the treatment that it looks amazing, even though I do actually say that myself. A totally extreme way of achieving this look and I categorically do not recommend it to anyone as I'm sure Clarins do   a very good night cream that is far less toxic than my current skin care regime, but a little something to add to my list of possible things that are good out of something bad. So far I have potentially amazing new boobs from Dan The Boob Man and Mr. Cautious Surgeon and new skin from Mr. Blinky Eyes, oh and of course no cancer from them all, that's sort of the most important one. Do I send them thank you cards when this is all done? Not sure that cuts it really.

21st July 2013

Jet lag and parties scuppered my Australian plans yesterday but all good things are worth waiting for and I get to see my favourite Aussie gorgeous girl tomorrow instead so all good. So me and Daisy partied hard at a summer garden party, the 1-year anniversary of the opening of The Sun, and blimey what a year its been. Daisy was used as child labour for the day as a very willing helper whilst painted as a butterfly and I caught up with friends I hadn't seen in a while.

So I found myself talking about all this nonsense for the first time in ages, out loud that is. I even threw in mine and Dave's breakup for good measure, you know just to wrap up the whole year with a big bow. Bizarrely I was at Dave's pub at the time as Daisy wanted to go and we are actually friends of which I am proud of myself for and it takes a lot for me to proud of myself. Julie who I was talking to said that last time she saw me I wasn't alright at all, that was in March whilst I was on that juggernaut to breakdownsville, but now I was much more, well like, me.

That got me thinking about my view of the world. I've had 2 views of the world. A cancer fuelled view and the Alex Jagger view. The cancer fuelled view has been dominating, no surprises there really but the Alex Jagger view is making lots of very welcome appearances. The cancer fuelled view is full of fear and insecurity, rash decisions and actions and a few pickles and scrapes and lots of stupidity. In fact, this view is exhausting and not the good kind. I can't count how many times various people have told me not to make   any decisions about anything just now, it dawned on me at around 4 am this morning why. I know I have said previously that I am a quick learner. I wasn't elaborating on the truth there because I promise I am. But, learning how to get through, around, over, under, whatever way you look at this thing that is cancer has been tricky.

The Alex Jagger view is coming back with a vengeance, full of the joys of what magic might happen now and especially once Dan The Boob Man and the rest of the band that are my consultants have finished making me whole again. It occurred to me that I don't need to wait for whatever I think I am waiting for and I can stop being scared of whatever I think I am scared of. Its time to trust in the 'premium care' (said by my dad channeled through Nessa (BF)) that I am getting and trust that they are making me better by the day and trust that I can start putting the cancer fuelled view away and just rely on that clear view of the world that is in fact my own. You know the saying 'life is not about waiting for the storm to pass but learning how to dance in the rain' I believe I may have been in a persistent hurricane to be fair, but I'm now starting to dance, as of about 3 days ago.

I'm not sure why or what happened and it only occurred to me in the early hours of this morning that something has in fact happened, but hey at least I got there. And before anyone gets any misguided ideas that I was drunk and that's why I was up in the early hours and being all philosophical, I wasn't sadly, just annoyingly couldn't sleep, nothing more exciting than that.

22nd July 2013

A bevy of beautiful babes, a gaggle of gorgeous girls or a lot of luscious lovely ladies all with the most amazing shoes was where it was at yesterday thanks to a

birthday and a super posh afternoon tea with very easy on the eye boys thrown in for good measure. Just what this girl needed and believe it should be made part of any treatment programme to hang out in such style.

So today, my Australian dreams become a reality and me and Daisy get to spend the day with Gaby, Bella and Saxon and we are super excited. I don't really care what we do but whatever we do I have leant that I need to take a hat with me. I have found that whenever the wind blows I am paranoid that my hair is literally going to blow off my head. I know that sounds crazy but I'm not going to get this far and let the weather add to my potential hair loss crisis. I don't want to go out on a windy day and then come back a few hairs lighter or worse, if there are any torrential down pours I dread to think what may happen. I will be known as the girl who beat cancer twice, averted hunch back and hair loss crisis, wasn't poisoned through bargaining with time debacle, who has found her mojo, got back into her groove but went out on a windy day and came back bald! I swear that when this is all over I am never going to complain about my hair ever, ever, ever. I am so unbelievably happy that my hair is still on my head, it means I can do things like go out as I did yesterday with people I don't really know feeling like me with no one none the wiser, unless they actually know of course!

But they didn't know because I looked like I wasn't having treatment for cancer because actually no one would know that from how I look and I am trying my best to keep it that way. So I need to get creative with hats as I'm not letting the weather get the better of me. My complaint about the weather is not of the usual kind as I love the hot sunny stuff, it's the windy stuff that is trying to steal my hair, its mine, leave it alone!

So, with the news full of royal babies and extreme weather my news is full of Australian dreams, gorgeous girls and having hair through extreme weather conditions. Apparently if the royal baby is a girl she will be called Alexandra and will be a Leo, I am called Alexandra and I am a Leo, so there you go. Does that mean I can be the Queen too. So, with mojo present and fully back in my groove, my rock and roll today is full of Australian gorgeousness. Cant wait!

23rd July 2013

So all is now well with the world as my gorgeous Aussie girl is back. Gaby, also known as my Hawaiian partner in crime, exhausted and worn out but most importantly back, hooray! Attingham Park was our place for the day, that was until Daisy got a little carried away with trying to swing herself on the swings that she pulled her muscles in her side, can't imagine where she gets that 'getting carried away' bit of determination from, mmm I wonder!

So, Tuesday is Grazia day, I never thought I would look forward to the postman quite this much for such a very shallow reason. Since the lovely Christine and Jayne bought me the Grazia subscription for my treatment, boy have I loved it! It's about as intellectual as it gets right now, but who needs more intellect on a Tuesday morning.

Anyway, a day at chez Jagger beckons today to get mine and Daisy's energy back. Getting back into ones' groove and finding that illusive mojo, or though not illusive any longer, takes some energy. We have a plan to do some jobs, Daisy's words by the way. She has a list. She is being quite bossy with this list. It may be a long day and I may be glad to hand her over to Dave at 4.30, you know only so she can get more jobs done with her daddy you understand.

So I have a very busy rock and roll day today with a 5-year- old very firmly in charge.

24th July 2013

The great escape, guinea pigs going AWOL or the big adventure, however I look at the day Amelia the guinea pig decided to make her bid for freedom. And boy can she move. She saw her opportunity and took it with huge determination. Hedgewood bound with her knapsack on her back.

So, I don't just have normal hedges in my garden as that would be too easy, I have the thickest, most over grown, prickly hedges going and there was no way me or Daisy were going to get in them or through them. Miss Daisy and me just looked at each other with no idea what to do. At this point I should really have been the grown up and had an instant plan but I was actually lost for how to get the little, scurrying, furry thing out of there. Daisy got her guinea pig book and told me to look at it to see if there was a section on what to do if they escape. There wasn't. So I went to the grown up for help that is the my Aussie favourite and she of course had a plan.

With apple and carrot trail in place me and Miss Daisy tip toed off to wait. And wait. And Wait. I had images of me waking up in the night with Ameila in the rain, on the road or in a cat's mouth. That in itself is a miracle as I am not an animal person. Much to Nessa's (Sisters) dismay. When it comes to animals I have nothing. Amelia and Lucy came to live with us as Daisy's treat for getting through the radiotherapy time. And for Daisy I will do anything. When I was diagnosed again I did worry that I might have to get more animals, that I would end up with a mini zoo. I   have luckily found other ways to get Daisy through it this time that has nothing to do with small living creatures.

We do however have 2 fish, Lexi and Luke. Whilst cleaning the tank out I left them in a bowl for 10 mins whilst me and Daisy sat down to wait for the tank water to settle. We heard a funny noise, did nothing. Then it carried on. I thought I better look. Luke had made a run for it and had jumped out of the bowl and was having a dance on the table, well I am sure it wasn't dancing but you know what I mean. That's how good I am with animals. Please note there were no animals harmed in the making of this story. Lexi and Luke live to tell another tale with a smile on their face.

Anyway, nothing happened for hours. I was now worried that we may never see Amelia again. I made up a great story for Daisy just in case, before we knew it Amelia had made it to the beach and was partying hard, sombrero on head and mojito in hand with lots of new furry friends to hang out   with. And then, out of the corner of my eye she was there, that little sniffy nose following the carrots and apples back to her hutch. Now I did at one point think Gaby was having a laugh with me about the trail, but it worked! Phew!

So, with all animals safely back where they should be and Miss Daisy happy once more it was time for her to head off for the night to leave me absolutely exhausted. And I mean so tired I could hardly move.

This is when I remember what I'm actually doing, you know having chemotherapy. Sometimes it's randomly easy to forget when I'm feeling good and sometimes out of the blue the tiredness hits me like a steam train. My temperature also started to creep up so it was time to take action as I'm not going to get myself an infection. So, I now have a plan for when this happens and I made a super powerful smoothie full of berries, yoghurt, manuka honey, spirulina, wheatgrass and cranberry juice. Drank the glass of green goodness and then juiced all the veg in the house I could get my hands on and went to bed.

My plan worked as my temperature has gone back down but my poor body is still so tired. So, today a massage beckons which I am very much looking forward to and then I need to not do very much, that is the very frustrating bit. My mind is so very active, who'd have thought that with me, ha! but my body sometimes doesn't want to play. A day of not doing very much, eating lots of super foods and I should be back to me again before long. The phrase 'you are what you eat' has never meant more to me than now. I can see the effects of food on my physical state, energy levels and my emotions to be honest like never before. It's almost like I have a little control over this, and it's always good to have a little control over having none at all.

So, my rock and roll today is coffee this morning with the lovely northern Jane and then a full body   massage. I don't think I have ever been more ready for this and I can't wait.

25th July 2013

Floating on a sea of Northern Jane'ness, full body massages and floristry was where it was at yesterday, oh and another guinea pig break out, clearly that guinea pig wants to be on the beach, shades on, mojito in hand partying hard and who can blame her.

It all started at Starbucks with Northern Jane, we laughed so much that I think they were quite glad to see us leave, around 3 hours of much laughter, I think that's quite perfect to be honest. Some may say we both like sharing our laughter with the world, we certainly did with Starbucks and all that sailed with her yesterday. A very good start to the day and I was very happy to be able to show off my hair and the fact that I still have it!

So then off for a massage. I've not had a massage for months and boy was I ready for it. I annoy myself a little whilst having massages normally as I try and work out what they are doing so I can pick up some tip. Not this time, I was away with those massaging fairies that were soothing my aching bones and enjoyed every minute of my hour of divine relaxation. Throughout my treatment so far my skin has become something quite amazing, an extreme way to get amazing skin, but all the same I'll enjoy it whilst it's here,

but the lady with magical massaging hands said the middle bit of me was a bit dry. I miss that bit out when using moisturiser on account of being scared I'm going to find something I don't want to find. In fact, I'd go as far as saying I cannot actually bring myself to moisturise neck down and waist up, it makes me want to cry so I don't do it. I'm fairly sure all is fine due to the toxic poison that kills all nasty's that may be lurking and also the fact that Dan The Boob Man is waiting in the wings to take this fear away from me.

I concluded that I will just have to have massages a lot so all my skin can be amazing without me having to freak myself out. Perfect! Next week is reflexology, magically massaged fairied feet beckons!

I floated away from my magical massage and got myself ready for all things flowers. The fabulously funky flowery Rachel taught us all how to make some cool flower designs, it was very very good and everyone managed to make some really cool flower arrangements. By the end of it though I was hit by that steam train of tiredness again and could hardly speak. I know, hard to believe. I got myself home and went to bed. The tiredness was so much that it felt like I was going under on anesthetic again. Dare I say that was quite nice! So dreamtastic sleep took over and was all consuming.

So, with amazing dreams giving me a spring in my step I am heading off for Aussie gorgeousness and seeing Gaby before

the joy that is my Oncologist appointment with Mr. Blinky Eyes. Daisy is staying with Gaby, I wouldn't put her through Mr. personality, and I'm Wolverhampton bound to see what my friendly Mr. Blinky Eyes has to say today. No doubt I will try to make him laugh and will probably fail miserably and I am definitely going to tell him he was wrong about my hair, well, he will be able to see for himself wont he. Aussie girls and Oncologist's is my rock and roll for the day with my amazing new song to spin and twirl around to courtesy of my lovely Abby.

ps. Amelia the guinea pig came back, smelling a little of cocktails and sun screen.

Alex Jagger

26th July 2013

Western Park, wasp stings, all things Australian and of course Mr. Blinky
Eyes was where it was at yesterday. The park and all things Australian
were the good parts of the day and the rest I think we could have done
without.

So, off to Western Park in Staffordshire which was great until a wasp
decided Gaby's arm looked tasty and decided to stick its little stinger in it.
Ouch! That was the point of no return for me as I had to leave her there
with ouchy arm and Miss daredevil Daisy

flying down every slide she could find then baring her pants to the world
in sheer excitement (like mother like daughter) to

go off and see Mr. Blinky Eyes.

Mr. Blinky Eyes does not improve with time, in fact I am quite sure his
people skills, or lack off, reached an all time high yesterday. Firstly, he
was late, that doesn't bother me at all. Only really the fact I had to sit in a
hospital a little longer and who likes being in hospitals when its sunny
outside. When it was my turn, he came to get me and then forgot which
room he was in, we went to 3 before he found his. This man has my life in
his hands!

His first words were 'I have no idea how you're keeping hold of your hair'.
Great! He then proceeds to tell me about how high grade, fast growing
and aggressive my cancer was, the heavy duty kind, it had grown 10 mm
in 4 months, that's very quick apparently. But my outlook was good,

about 89% chance of non reoccurrence in the next 10 years with all the treatment and surgery. Breast cancer has a nasty habit of coming back more than other types, he said. No shit Sherlock I thought. He corrected himself once realising that it had already come back, although he did say it was probably there at the same time as the first one even though its classed as a 2nd occurrence and also that surgery will take that risk practically away, so my outlook was really good.

He then finished that particular line of chat by telling me I will go into remission and when I get to 4 to 5 years I can consider myself cured. I think this was good news, so why did I feel like it wasn't? Maybe its all in the delivery.

So, he was happy with my progress and how I am coping with this super high dose I am on and I get to not see him for another 6 weeks, woo woo! That will be just before my 5th cycle, that means by then I am nearly finished. So I leave and as I go I say that I hope I still have my hair next time I see him. To that he laughed, a lot. In fact, the most I have ever seen him laugh. Not sure he believes that will happen as it seems I'm defying the odds already on that front. And I intend to carry on.

In the car and out of that hospital as quick as I can, I cry all the way back to Gaby's, puzzled by my reaction to this meeting as I'm all good with what's going on. I get there and Gaby manages to pick me up off the floor and gets me back to some sort of normality and we both conclude that its just been a while since I have had to talk about it in such official and scary terms. And she said I would be a freak of human nature if I didn't get big wobbles about it from time to time. I agreed.

We then had another hair chat. Ms. gorgeous Aussie girl had some pearls of wisdom and we settled on the fact I still have it, why wouldn't I keep it now even though every cycle is a new battle on the hair crisis.

Worse case I lose it but at least by the end of October it will start growing back and I won't have not had it for the whole treatment. See, positive. Most importantly me and my hair are still happily living together in blissful harmony.

So as long as I remain coping as I am with the treatment nothing changes and I get a 6 week break from Mr. Blinky Eyes. That's incentive enough to remain as robust as I clearly am. Onwards and upwards, off that floor again and back doing this the only way I know how. That would be my way.

So today, Daisy has gone out with Northern Jane, Robert and Charlotte to look for deer at Attingham Park and I am finally doing a lot of things that desperately need doing that are admin'y boring type stuff but things that will make a life time of difference, or is that a difference to the rest of my life time, whatever I just gotta do them. I am taking advantage of the fact I can use my brain today, finally!

Then a visit from Julie, Evie and Charlie to finish off the day and 2 treats for me from myself. Flowers and mojito marmalade!

27th July 2013

Wanting to take a leaf out of Amelia the guinea pigs book and come home smelling a little of mojitos and sun screen, I had mojito marmalade on my toast and then twirled and spun around with Daisy in the in the kitchen to my new favourite song from Abby. A perfect start to the day and the perfect way to make sure my mojo is still

in its groove, which it is again. Had a Mr. Blinky Eyed blip yesterday but all is right with the world again today, can't beat a good Miss Daisy dance to get back into your groove.

So we are now well and truly into the Witches of Eastwick birthday season. One very drunk night out many years ago myself, Nessa (BF) and Abby decided we were in fact the Witches of Eastwick. Lots of magic going on clearly and we believed it was very funny at the time. It all starts tomorrow with Nessa, then me and then Abby all in the next 4 weeks. I have a sneaky feeling mine may be a little tame this year on account of toxicity and mojitos not mixing very well but you never know, I may yet pull off some kind of celebration. Nessa of course is doing hers in style today and I can't go, absolute bummer! I'm there is spirit!

I am in fact going to another party, of the child variety at the lovely Christine's amazing house today with Miss Daisy, of course or that would a little odd!

And I am going with a head full of possibilities and how I can bargain with time again! I'm not proposing to anyone that I speed up my treatment as I know

I would never actually get to the end of it on account of probably being poisoned and I don't want to be known as the girl who survived cancer twice, averted hunch back and potential hair loss crisis but was poisoned through bargaining

with time debacle, that really would be rubbish after all this. I have tried to spin it to see how I can make it feel like October isn't that far away! Here is how I have done it so far.

Today birthday season starts for 4 weeks and Daisy is off school and so far I am ok to do stuff when I have her. And I have loads of amazing people to hang out with. When she goes back to school I will only have 4 weeks left and in that time I see Mr. Blinky Eyes, Mr. Cautious Surgeon and Dan The Boob Man so I will be busy ish with them. Also, next week I am half way through. When on holiday for 2 weeks the first week goes slowly and the second week goes really fast so if that theory works with chemotherapy then after next week it should fly by.

So, taking away the poisoning fiasco I think I would rather be known as the girl who survived cancer twice, averted hunch back crisis, defied all logic by keeping her hair, had a head full of possibilities, as well as hair and who couldn't keep her guinea pigs from escaping to party.

In fact, I think I would rather be known just as the girl who always has a head full of possibilities, on account of as soon as this is over I am putting all this away in the box

that is marked 'life changing and never to do again'. What ever I am known as I'll never be able to stop the guinea pigs from partying, in fact I'll be the one coming home with the aroma of fully fledged mojitos and sun screen whilst they look on in awe.

28th July 2013

I missed my vocation in life. I should have been a politician as it seems I can put a spin on most things to make them appear better than they actually are. I think the trick is believing the spin, today I have not. The spin I am referring to is of course about time. How to make time appear to speed up to get to October quicker than a snail pace. I'm not good with waiting and patience, I think I have made that quite apparent throughout.

I'm also not good at waiting to be wiped out every 3 weeks, it all seems so bizarre at times. Although in 4 days I will be half way through, that sounds good. This is the biggest lesson I hope I ever have to learn about being patient. I am now more patient than ever, even though that appears to be a little bit of a contradiction to what I have just said.

So, today is Nessa's (BF) birthday. I wish more than anything I was in Leeds right now celebrating with her but we are going to save a lot of celebrating for October.

We will be celebrating all of our birthdays, the end of chemotherapy and the fact my sanity remained throughout, ready for Dan The Boob Man to work his magic. I can't wait! But I'm a little sad that I can't be there now and it makes me a little sad remembering why I'm not there. In fact, all it makes me think is that this is all a bit rubbish at times. But that's' also ok, as it is rubbish however I spin the cancer stuff, there is no way to look at that to make it alright, apart from the fact I don't have it any longer of course.

So the champagne is on ice.

Anyway, it seems someone has hidden my mojo as I can't seem to find it. I think I'm still in my groove as I've sort of hit my 'f**k it' button and thrown caution to the wind to push myself a bit to go hunting for this illusive mojo. I'm sure it won't be far, in fact I bet Daisy took it out with her. Whatever, it will turn up and I will be back to the determined girl that I know and love in no time.

I've got nothing more today apart from to wish the most gorgeous Nessa a very very happy happy birthday!x She is taking care of the rock and roll today!

29th July 2013

Beetroot juice. That's what I've been dealing with most

of today, it gets everywhere when a crafty elbow knocks a whole pint of the stuff off from the kitchen table, fennel included of course. My kitchen is white, normally anyway. Today It looks as though I've taken to mass murder. Daisy found it hilarious. Me not so.

So, it seems Daisy did take my mojo out with her yesterday as when she came back this morning all was fine again. After throwing caution to the wind yesterday by hitting my 'f**k it' button I felt slightly liberated and a bit more accepting of my current chemo fuelled circumstances realising that I can't actually do anything about it. Days like yesterday are actually good, that button should be pressed more often, although yesterday I'm not sure I would have agreed as I think that button usually has consequences. So my determined cautious optimism has returned for now, rightly or wrongly, what will be will be and all that nonsense but at least today I feel like I can see the finishing line. I still have my eye on the prize and that prize is holding a bottle of champagne with my name on it.

Anyway, slightly exhausted from all my emotion yesterday I was quite happy to hear the thunder and see the rain, me and Miss Daisy sat outside and watched and listened for ages and of course got very wet. And when the sun came out with a vengeance we went searching for fairies, as you do.

Catriona the amazing cake maker has a lot to answer for when it comes to going to the park as now we have to search for fairy dust. Catriona plants this in advance like any good fairy dust keeper does. It seems I am not a fairy dust keeper and had none to hand so had to try and persuade Miss Daisy we must have been too late and it all must have gone. She didn't buy it. We kept on looking until the park was about to close and luckily hunger took over and we haven't mentioned fairies since.

So, on Thursday I will be half way through as long as all is good with my blood tests on Wednesday. It does feel good being able to say half way through. And August is nearly upon us and I have 2 treatments in August as well as a birthday so it's not all bad. Here I go bargaining with time again.

So my rock and roll today has been beetroot fuelled mass murder, thunder, illusive fairy dust and the welcome return of my mojo.

30th July 2013

Carrot cake, crafty kids, Catriona 'The Classy Cake Baker' and fancy foot work has been my day. I managed to avoid the mass murder of the previous day and kept all the beetroot juice confined to my mouth as opposed to the kitchen, which is now white again and needs to stay that way.

Me and Miss Daisy managed to get out of the house somehow dressed and in some sort of orderly fashion to wing our way to Catriona's house for a day of frivolity and cakes. Catriona makes the best cakes in the world and she has taken to making me one every time I see her. I am taking this as another 'good out of something' bad element of all this as these cakes are gorgeous beyond belief.

Once there it feels like time flies and I leave on my own to go for my fancy foot work in the form of reflexology. I have been looking forward to this as much as my day with Catriona, nothing like the Classy Cat, cake and a good foot rub to sort you out. Now, I think I am quite good at all things feet myself, but I have to say I now know I am a mere amateur. An hour of pleasure and pain is the best way to describe it, in a nice way of course. The bits that hurt were my solar plexus meaning I'm out of balance emotionally. Shocker! Followed by my liver, kidneys and lymph nodes, all the parts that flush out toxins and as I am currently toxic Jagger that makes perfect sense. She then said I was really healthy. How ironic! So, I now have a thumping headache and a stiff neck, no idea why, and am about ready for bed at the ripe old time of 8pm. ROCK AND ROLL! She did say this would happen to me. And I have booked again for next week, am I mad?

So back to Catriona's where Daisy is having a ball.

A lovely, chilled out afternoon followed, just what I needed. And of course amazing cake. Whilst there the nurse calls me to arrange to take my blood tomorrow to make sure I'm good for Thursday. And there it is. The reason I am doing what I'm doing giving me a slap in the face again. However much I dread treatment day it's a necessary evil and I will be so pissed off if it doesn't happen on time, to my planned schedule. Let's hope I've recovered ready to get past my half way mark. Please.

So there we have it, I'm on the countdown for no.3. Nessa (BF) is heading my way tomorrow to take my mind off what's coming and Nessa (sister) is off duty this time to save her driving half way across the country through her peak season in Cornwall. The gorgeous Gaby is keeping me company throughout my treatment on Thursday and then I'm flying solo through the worst of it.

Una from The Saturdays thinks I will recover quicker this way. Let's see if she is right. Daisy will be away and luckily I have lots of people just a stones throw away just in case I run out of something I think I can't live without.

So my rock and roll today has been filled with the Classy Catriona, kids, carrot cake, fancy foot work and   the earliest night in the word. Sweet dreams....

31st July 2013

So, we are on. 10am tomorrow Una from The Saturdays will be winging her way to me with all of her needles and   toxic nonsense to get me past the half way point. Not sure if I am happy or not really but at least I'm getting to tick these off and get closer the finishing line, you know champagne on ice and of course the end of chemotherapy, I cannot wait like I have never wanted something so much in my life.

In the spirit of keeping my eye on the prize, Nessa and me decided on the 25th October as the date for our champagne weekend to celebrate the end of treatment pre surgery. It's in the diary and a very good focus for me, that's 12 weeks and 2 days, not that I'm counting or anything. That means that my last treatment is 9 weeks' tomorrow. The words time and bargaining spring to mind.

Today me and Miss Daisy drove each other a little around the twist with it being a rainy day and the day before chemo is always a little tense for me, until Nessa (BF) arrived and then she was driving her around the twist as well. Jane the nurse popped in to do all the pre chemo checks, Daisy watched with a weird fascination at my blood being taken whilst Nessa and me looked way. Such grown ups.

So, now I am doing my normal nervous, butterflies in tummy stuff ready for tomorrow. No painting tonight thank goodness as Nessa is here to stop me, we are settling for rubbish TV and our usual AlJag and Nessa behaviour so all good. So this is me for now. I'll be back on the other side of my half way point.

So my rock and roll today has been Miss Bossy Boots, my gorgeous Nessa (BF) and butterflies, not bad for the day before no.3.

PS.. Celebrity Master chef started tonight, one of my favs! We decided that due to our extensive culinary skills, Ness would be making Jacket potato and salad and I would be making chilli, that's how good we are.

2nd August 2013

So, today I am closer to the end of this than I am the beginning, just by a day, but what a difference day   makes! Hooray for getting past the half way point. I am feeling super sick but am doing just fine. To say it's just the day after I am getting up every now and again, this is one of my again times, and then sleeping lots which I think is doing it right. The lovely Christine came to see me for a couple of hours which was great until I hit my wall and had to go to bed.

Yesterday, of course was a sightly different picture. Nessa (BF) was here and the gorgeous Gaby also, they kept me sane and emotionally in the right place until Una from The Saturdays got here with her needles and off it started   again.

The drugs bit is the easy bit, but the cold cap was very hard yesterday. It made me feel sick and freezing cold. So when it was one of the hottest days outside I was wrapped up in a jumper, blanket and woolly socks and my lips were   blue. But I got through it with the help of Gaby rubbing my feet and hands in a true reflexology style which   was wonderful, I did say it was love when your mate does that whilst wired up.

So not much to report today apart from I am again over whelmed at the love of those all around me wanting to do anything they can to help me, I'm safe in the knowledge Miss Daisy is having fun in Cheltenham and that I can welcome Nessa (BF) back tomorrow as a surprise visit before her hols which is just fantastic. Oh, and I've taken to watching Magnum P.I. I had forgotten how good it was.

So, my rock and roll today will be spent mainly sleeping with a bit of Magnum PI, I think that sounds wrong but you know what I mean. Another good reason to go to Hawaii though.

3rd August 2013

So, here I am, day 3 into my half way point and doing ok.

I've been flying solo this time around which has been just   fine. I've managed to do everything I have needed to

do, you know like feed myself and get water and sleep, lots of sleep. I have not felt vulnerable in anyway so I am very happy with myself.

It sounds so basic really but when feeling quite so rough I am mighty happy that I am up, bathed, fed and watered and almost dressed. I have my big bi fold doors open and am enjoying the fresh air. So now I just need to stay still and I will feel ok! Nessa (BF) is winging her way to me as we speak for a surprise visit which is just perfect as I wont see her until September, arrghh! By the time I see her again I will have done cycle 4 and will be 1 week off cycle 5. In fact, 2 months today is my last cycle as long as I stay to plan. Time and bargaining spring to mind again.

I think I am quite lucky that I completely forget how bad it is for the first 2 days of each cycle, the cold cap especially, that was mighty tough this time. I can really see why people stop using them half way through, of course I am going to try very hard to carry on, but not at the detriment of my well being it has to be said. I will take it one cycle at a time as the longer it goes on the longer I have hair and what ever happens it will start growing back in October anyway. At least I will have hair for my birthday and that was one of my secret goals, that is 2 weeks today.

I just have to remember that each day it gets better after treatment day, its hard to remember that when feeling like this, but I know I will get there.

I've got to the top of that mountain I have been climbing and I'm on the way down the other side. I'm sure it's part physiological as well as the more I think it was ok last time the more I think it will be this time, if your told something will be worse, it usually is. I have been up in bed chatting to the gorgeous Gaby and gin Jayne, on the phone of course or it would have been a bit of a squeeze, and have done well talking, as it sounds funny but yesterday I couldn't talk without feeling sick.

So all good and positive.

So my rock and roll today is of course filled with Nessa (BF) and not moving much. Perfect.

ps. I'll try and sneak a bit of Magnum PI into the rock and roll day too!

<u>4th August 2013</u>

Today is friendship day so it was a perfect day to be with Nessa (BF).

Actually any day to be with her is a perfect day and it was super perfect that she winged her

way to me for the night yesterday to hang out with me in my very rock and roll way of not moving much from the sofa. There's not many people you can just do nothing with as well as we can, there are a few but me and Nessa do it very well!

So yesterday was a good day, spent with Nessa and a visit from Miss Daisy so we could get our fix. She's coming   home tomorrow and I cannot wait! I ate Nessa's Masterchef special of jacket potato and salad and stayed up well into the night, and by that I mean 10pm! Funnily this morning I woke up at 4.44am whereas yesterday it was 3.33am, I am wondering if I will get to 5.55am tonight. I of course went back to sleep; I have learnt I can do that this time around which is a bit of a relief. No more midnight painting or watching silly films back to back in the night. Not at the moment anyway.

Anyway, it seems Una from The Saturdays was right, getting my independence back through these first few days has been good and I have coped well, I got a good start with Nessa (sister) getting me established but now I think I may be OK to fly solo apart from the day of actual treatment as it's nice to have someone to chat to whilst that little treat is going on. I feel quite good about that as does everyone else as it means it's not beating me and I now know it won't. However tired I feel. And that's' because I am one lucky girl. Friendship day and all that, it should be renamed friendship year for me.

So, I am on day 4 today and I have been up, dressed and have been out for lunch with Nessa and Miss Daisy which was a very nice treat. I am now so tired I can hardly move but I did manage a walk in the park with gin Jayne in the pouring rain which was lovely. And now I really can't move.

I have a banging headache still from the cold cap and my sickness comes and goes but is going more than coming which is the way I like it.

The cold cap thing is terrifying me now; I am getting flash backs already about how it makes me feel. I am going to reserve judgment on that as the days go by to see if I can forget how bad it was, along with the treatment which is bad enough. The treatment is hard, trust me on this, I hope no one reading this ever has to do it. Add treatment to the cold cap and it feels a little like torture at the moment. I can't believe I am going to say this but I'm a little over my hair, I just want to get through the next 3 cycles and it means more to me to get through it than keep my hair. What a difference a cycle makes! I may change my mind; I'm allowed to I think.

So, I am beyond tired, my brain isn't working and I need to do nothing. NOW! That's how rock and roll I am. Somebody stop me!

Alex Jagger

5th August 2013

Wobbly teeth, sore veins, weird chemo head bubble and

glitter is where it's at today. Miss Daisy is home with big news….. her first wobbly   tooth! It's clearly a momentous day. But this only happened later in the day, before that it wasn't as much fun, apart from the glitter of course.

Not much fun as I felt dreadful. My veins are so bruised and sore in my arms, I dread to think what I look like, but   more importantly it's how I feel, and that is dreadful. Flat as that pancake I can't manage to flip, in a very weird chemo funny world that no one else gets into, I don't like it very much. So to try desperately to get myself out of it, me and Miss Daisy go out and buy all things glitter to make when we get home. Mission accomplished, house full of glitter but no real lift in my head, my very sore head that is. Miss Daisy is fine, very happy actually as the whole tooth thing happened and we have managed to be very creative all day without moving very much which is perfect for me.

So, sore head and weird head bubble, neither very nice. Sore head due to the torturous cold cap. I have today booked an appointment at Toni&Guy as they do a specialist wig service and I figured they may do good ones. It's only just in case I can't do the cold cap anymore, I won't decide until the day but I need a contingency plan, and a very good short wig may just do the job for the 2 months I may not have hair.

Three more treatments with a cold cap feels like another mountain to climb, three more without feels like I can do it.

That's quite a big deal and my head is still very sore now 5 days on. And I have to remember that really no one else cares if I have hair or not, I have no one to impress, no big events after my birthday is done, not that it's really a big

event, I will no doubt be asleep before anything exciting happens! Even Miss Daisy is quite excited about the thought of me with no hair. Maybe its just part of the whole thing, you know, having no hair. And the weird head space thing, not sure where that's come from, but super paranoia creeps in and I don't appreciate it!

To save the day, the lovely Beccy came by and took me out of my weird head bubble and put me back on an even keel, just with herself, seems that's all it takes. A cup of tea and a chat and lovely mojito mix for my birthday (non alcoholic) is just perfect! So I guess to look on the good side of life today, I have been out, driven my car, made all things glitter, hung out with Beccy and sort of entertained Miss Daisy, I'm not sure I was doing this last cycle, so that has to be good news.

So my rock and roll tonight will no doubt will be filled with wobbly teeth, and that's just fine!

ps. I woke up at 5.55am this morning. 4.44am day before and 3.33am the day before that. no kidding!

6th August 2013

'That's a rock and roll name'....

stopped me in my tracks   today. If only the woman knew what that meant to me at the moment! So my rock and roll started early, with my name as it happened and maybe a

good omen for what I was doing at the time, who knows.

Anyway, the day started today with breakfast in bed. Miss Daisy made tea and toast and I can say hand on heart it actually tasted mighty fine. A good start to the day especially with a very sore head still. The second good bit of the day was a visit from Jo, Sian and Sam which was lovely. Daisy and Sian have clearly been separated at birth as I've not seen two little monkeys quite so similar, it was fascinating and it was good to catch up.

We decided to let the universe take over, not that we would ever relinquish any responsibility you understand, but sometimes, surely there have to be stronger forces at work. Slightly cosmic? Maybe, Clutching at straws? Very possibly! The third good bit of the day was Pizza Express with Dave, Daisy, Gin Jayne and James, perfect and very very tasty.

So, the fourth good bit of the day is that I'm tired out from the first three good bits. Too tired for my sore head to work. So, my very rock and roll day has all been in my name today, pizza and of course the universe.

ps. I have my Toni&Guy hair loss consultation thing tomorrow in conjunction with Macmillan. It's for 2 hours, I wonder what they do, stick it back on!

<u>7th August 2013</u>

Gentle James the hair man, feet, glimmers of gold and feeling slightly better about the whole damn shooting match is where its at today. Despite writing many, wondrous words about how I am feeling since this began, I still haven't been able to find the right words to describe how I actually feel. But there are times when I get a sense of how I feel, like a glimmer of seeing something through the muddy waters that sparkles and catches my eye, and my heart, and then it goes. Like trying to catch mist. These little glimmers are the best bits. The moments of clarity that make me feel like I'm getting through. I had one today. Whilst sat with the very gorgeous Gaby and telling her about gentle James the hair man, I just said very casually that my treatment is over in less than 2 months. Sounds very simple, I know, but I think I may have just seen the end of the treatment in my head. That's a first.

So, gentle James made me feel a whole lot better about my hair. He knew all about the cold cap torture, my treatment and what happens with my hair and head.

My scalp   is inflamed it seems, hence the pain, this has noting to do with the cold cap, it's the treatment.

I can't see it but he could and he put something on to sooth it which it has done already. He cut my hair, bizarre really but there you go and he said my hair is looking good, no bald patches (always good) and the cap is really working. Maybe I should try and carry on with it. Let's see if I can, I will try. My hair looks no different to before my treatment began despite loosing some, amazing really. It may have just given me the encouragement I needed.

So - just stepped out of a salon hour later - I go for all things feet. My reflexology hour of pleasure and pain. Una from The Saturdays is insistent that I treat my whole self, not just with chemotherapy but with massage, nutrition and general well being. I agree with her and have vowed to do as much as I can within reason, even if I don't want to. I say this after just drinking a pint of fennel and vegetable juice. If I never drink fennel juice again after this is over, it will be too soon.

The same bits flag up this week as they did last time with my feet which is no surprise, but I think it may have done some good, mind over matter and all that.   Anyway, with all the excitement of glimmering moments, hair cuts and painful feet I am absolutely exhausted. Miss Daisy is on safari tomorrow so I have a day to get some energy back as I feel like I've left my mojo at the hairdressers.

So, all that glimmers is gold has been my rock and roll today... but now this crazy cat needs to sleep.

8th August 2013

Ok universe, reveal yourself! Its time to show me   what you're made of. The good, the bad and the ugly. I think I'm doing the bad and I've done the ugly so I am now holding out for the good. Surely its time. Well, I'm saying it's time, so if you're listening, bring it on. NOW!

A little bored is where its at a little today, shocker!

A sign that I'm coming round and a sign that I can't actually believe its only August. Yesterday I was raving about my glimmer of gold. Today, it's a distant memory. I am so fickle. Time is playing games with me again, probably due to my fickleness, maybe I'm teasing time. Now there's a thought.

So, whilst attempting to do something constructive I looked through some books. If they haven't got pictures in right now I'm buggered as I can't focus long enough to read a sentence, very annoying, but I found a lame attempt at a diary earlier in the year that I had written. I managed 2 days! Clearly I had no focus then either. I think that was to do with shock of getting cancer in the first place and heading for breakdownsville over chemotherapy brain.

I scared myself reading it. It was the day before flippin pancake day and the day itself and it was an absolute disaster.

Or I was an absolute disaster. By that I mean I was in such a bad place. I wish I could have seen myself through my eyes now back then as I would have given myself a good talking to and then a very big cuddle. I'm not surprised I stopped writing it. But I am rather pleased I keep getting little reminders that I have actually come a long way and even at my weakest moments, they are not as weak as then. Phew!

Anyway, today this crazy cat is full of catitude to bring on, well just something. I have eaten tasty burgers with Dave and mildly put the world to rights with the very gorgeous Gaby and feel a little spring in my step, especially in comparison to Miss 'I'm trying really hard to pretend I'm ok but really I'm in agony inside' from flippin pancake day above. So all is not bad, I may still have a funny feeling head and am super tired and have very little concentration, but I'm doing just fine.

So, my rock and roll today has been full of catitude, bringing on the 'good' and tasty burgers and long may it continue.

9ᵗʰ August 2013

Miss Daisy, manicures, pyjamas, neighbours and beating the boredom is where its been at today, oh and letting the universe do its stuff, of course.

I said I was ready for the good, remember, I'm still ready. I shall reserve judgment and try and hold my nerve so I don't get too carried away and scare the good fairies from my door, not like me I know, but then again this is a whole new world now.

So, my day started with Miss Daisy painting my nails. Not only was I left with a very interesting set of sort of painted nails and fingers, I had to pay for it, along with my tea and toast. So, 23p later, very good value, we had a flurry of excitement whilst planning our escape from Wem, more on that later, but it felt a little like something good was happening. Myself and Miss Daisy managed to stay in our pyjamas most of the day until we were forced to leave the house, she kept busy dong all things glitter and I did a very good job of supervising as today I have been super tired with unbelievably sore veins.

This is where I beat the boredom as I was too tired for a start and I googled sore veins and how to stop them in between clearing up split glitter and making bracelets and headbands, as you do. Lots of water and miso soup apparently stop the vein   issue, slightly random but I'll give anything a go.

So, back to the great escape. My lovely neighbour Kate popped by, or Mate as Daisy calls her, to plot the mass exodus from the desirable end of Wem.

It was news to the pair of us that there was in fact a desirable part of Wem, but apparently there is and we are in it. So it seems we have all decided it's time to fly the nest and spread our wings. We may have to find a house next door to Mate and Kel (Kate and Mel) again as they are too nice to leave. Stalker behaviour? Very possibly! The general consensus in my head and of those around me is that it may be too difficult to move on in this house after everything and it may be time, after my treatment and surgery of course, to find a new home for me and Miss Daisy, a nice fresh, free from cancer and divorce and chemotherapy house to make our home, to fill full happy times and glitter.

This house also needs to be in a much more happening place. I'm not a stay at home person at the best of times. 2013 will be known, amongst other things, as the year I stayed at home so as soon as all this nonsense is over we will be out as much as we can be, doing as much as we can, so a place with good things to do, would be a good start.

So, back to the universe showing its stuff, I am at the mercy of the house selling and buying fairies to find me the perfect house at the perfect time. I don't ask for much do I! So, the keeper of my heart, Miss Daisy finished off the day by painting my toes and charging me 32p for the pleasure. I am very glad I am having a birthday pedicure treat next week is all I am saying.

So, my very tired rock and roll has been filled with nail varnish, dreaming of brighter, glittering futures and of course stalking my neighbours.

10th August 2013

Today is mainly full of desire. Desire for things I cannot have right now. Nothing too extravagant you understand, I'm not playing the lottery game of what I would have if I won a zillion pounds.

No, its things that are breaking my heart.

My long hair, today I hate my short hair with a passion and I know that sounds borderline insane as I actually have hair which is a massive, massive, massive thing, but just today I want my long hair back.

Energy. I have none. I don't like it.

Brain power. I have none. I feel stupid.

My soulmatetypeperson, unspecified but missing.

Lightheartedness, missing in action along with my mojo. I have no idea what my groove looks like as I'm certainly not in it.

Today I am pissed off with the whole damn shooting match. I'm teetering on the edge of an almighty cavern and I'm having all on stopping myself from falling. This is truly rubbish. It will pass. I know.

So, I dabbled in a little stalking and went to see Kate next door for a coffee, that got me out of my horriblness for a while which was good. Miss Daisy nearly spun herself off a chair and I had visions of beautiful items being smashed   to smithereens, luckily Kate has Miss Daisy's number which works a treat. So back to trying to get through the day, I won't harp on about it as it even bores me and I'm the one with this pain inside that just will not go away. This is what I have done:

- Watch terrible celeb TV about the worst divorces ever, it made me laugh, they're all nutters;

- Made chicken curry and baked a cake;

- Drank a glass of red wine, oh how I have missed a   little red wine;

- Went for hot chocolate at my favourite hot chocolate   shop with Miss Daisy;

- Hugged Daisy until she got bored of it and told me to go away;

• Remembered that I don't have cancer and that this is really important to make sure I never have it again.

So there we have it. I'm no crazy cat today, more like an ostrich with my head down hiding. I'll be happy when this pain goes from inside, please, sometime soon would be good.

So, my rock and roll today has been of the melancholic variety. Bring back the golden sunshine.

11th August 2013

Sorry. I'll start with that now as I haven't got anything good to say today. I wasn't going to write anything but if I don't I am forgetting why I started doing this in the first place. I began writing this to remember how I feel through this most terrible of times for me, for Daisy if she ever wants to know in the coming years and to stop me online shopping. So, in the spirit of that, I shall write a little, not a lot as no one wants to read about sadness.

I have a pain inside, it is all consuming and I don't know how to stop it. It's the horrible pain that reminds me that cancer has the ability to devour every inch of you and can destroy lives and destroy souls.

My life will not be destroyed by it as I will be getting through this with my health intact. It's my soul I'm a little concerned about at the moment.

I have been rocked to my very core and sometimes I have no idea how to come back from it. These last few days have been

tricky. I am beyond tired and beyond logical reason. In fact, I don't even know what logical reason means today.

On these days it seems that every advert on TV is about cancer, no one should face cancer alone they all say. But we do. No one sees my dark moments of sheer pain and   fear. I'm very lucky with the amount of people around me in my very unconventional but amazing set up of friends and family, neighbours, ex husband and of course the keeper of my heart Miss Daisy and I am far from alone but sometimes I have to be alone to get through the reality of it.

The intensity of this - that is spread over so many months is sometimes exasperating, I have been doing this for 8 months already and have more months just spreading out in front of me. Most of the time I can get my head around that, today I can't and I feel mighty angry at the world and angry that I am having to do this. I can also remember that it's not going to kill me so I haven't lost my complete grasp of reality just yet. I can see all the positive stuff, more than most people can, but there are days when no amount of my usual upbeat, lighthearted, logical, strong ways can make sense of this.

If and when I get through this with all my faculties intact, I may just be invincible. I'm far from that place right now.

Tomorrow is another day and today is nearly over, especially as I'm going to have the earliest night in this crazy rock and roll life of mine. I will carry on putting one foot in front of the other and will wait for the fog to lift for me to get back to my fighting self.

That me has just popped out for a bit of a break, probably spinning and twirling around somewhere with a mojito in hand. That's my girl!

So, I was right to start by saying sorry, not the greatest of days. Not even the David Beckham ad has put a smile on my face, that's bad.

No rock and roll today.

ps. I could just turn the TV off. As I can't read yet and I have the energy of a person with none, TV is all I can muster.

pps. It would be wrong to stop online shopping completely, especially with a birthday looming.

12th August 2013

I'm back. From the depths of my despair that is.

I've said it before and I am sure I will say it again, we all have bad days, I just write about mine and let people into a world that I   would normally keep well hidden.

I'm not keeping it well hidden this time around as last time I did that I had a rather fast and treacherous journey to breakdownsville and

that particular holiday destination didn't score well on trip advisor, in fact it states 'not recommended, very poor standards and definitely no repeat visits.'

So, a bit of a roller coaster all of this nonsense, I have figured out it's probably harder to deal with emotionally than physically due to the intensity, time, lack of mental ability, lack of control and just the sheer fact that I'm being pushed to every limit I've ever had and now beyond into unknown territory. Unknown territory however, can be   a mixture of fear and excitement.

 The last few days have been fear, you may have gathered! But little bits of excitement creep in, mainly when I'm thinking about the end of it!

Seven weeks on Thursday is my last treatment day, facts like that are my little glimmers of gold that keep me going. I'll deal with what's next on this journey when I get past the 3rd October. There's one thing I am sure about; it can't be worse than this!

On the lack of control thing, gorgeous Gaby today did say that I could do with trying to stop needing a reason for everything, in other words trying to control it. It drives me mad if I can't find a reason for how I'm feeling.

If you understand something, you can control how you feel about it, knowledge is power and all that. I may be emerging as a slight control freak here, but we rested on this being another learning curve. Maybe she's right, maybe she's not. Maybe it's hard to call unless you've walked my walk. But boy - I am so over learning curves and being told how to behave − try my shoes for size first please − then you can give me your opinion.

Anyway, today has been about the lovely Rachel and gorgeous Beatrice and Una from The Saturdays and of course the very lively Miss Daisy. So firstly we had a visit from Rachel and Beatrice which was so lovely. Rachel has been on this same journey I am currently on and she was one of the only people I spoke to who had been through cancer that I wanted to talk to when it happened to me, the other being Lindsay. It's a strange thing, I couldn't talk to anyone else who had been through it - I could have been told something that scared me more - although I'm not sure that was possible at the time, but all the same, I thought it could so I put my hands over my ears and did the 'la la la' song. Nothing like a bit of denial!

I still can't talk to other people who have been there really, just in case. It is good though to be with someone who just knows exactly what its like, and that's what today was like, I didn't have to explain anything, she just knew. Perfect! Beatrice was on great form, as it seems was Miss Daisy.

So I got to catch up about work too which seems a million miles away but good all the same.   Una from The Saturdays came to do my toxicity visit. She again seemed to see into my soul and she was relieved that I was alright and that I still had hair! I did enlighten her on my hair journey over the last week and she was happy that I'm a determined girl - we've come this far and all that. She thinks the inflammation on my scalp could well have been ice burn, nice!

So we have a plan for next week to make it a little more bearable that I feel happy with. Ten days, a birthday, some great days planned with lots of different people and I reach cycle number four and the thought of six weeks left fills me with utter joy.

So, my mojo is heading my way, it's been having a spin   and twirl and the odd mojito in my absence, and who could blame it! I can see my groove and as soon as I get some more sleep I will be doing my best to get like Madonna and get back into it.

So, my rock and roll, which has resumed full service you will be pleased to know, today has been full off fabulous friends, control freaks and more blooming learning curves. I still say bring back the golden sunshine, I want to bask in its warm glow.

13th August 2013

So, the lovely Jo came over with her super cool kids Sian and Sam and we got a fix of our rightmove addiction and the very gorgeous Gaby and equally cool kids Bella and Saxon came over so the house was full of lovely people which is just what we needed. Of course Daisy managed to argue with all of them and spent most of the day crying. We all have those days, she is so like me, minus the arguing that is, I just do the crying.

Mass exodus including Miss stoppy pants who stropped off with her dad and left me to my own devices. A little quiet time with a whole bag of pop corn and a lot of blue cheese and biscuits, no idea why, but it tasted good.

Looking forward to my birthday pedicure treat and massage tomorrow, I can't promise I will stay awake through it but I am sure it will be just what it's called, a treat. And we all like treats.

So, my rock and roll today has been yet again of the tired variety but with lots of lovely people to entertain me in the process.

14th August 2013

Glorious feet, super soothing back massages, dinner with two

lovely boys and a spring in my step is where its been at today. And a rather late night for Miss Jagger it has to be said, crazy!

Energy in abundance of which has completely been taken advantage of, it has been unusually gratifying to be on my feet nearly all day, well apart from the mega relaxing massages going on of course, they may have spurred me on just a little.

So, my birthday treat of all things feet and backs was the start of my day, and what a start to the day. I was transported to a soft and fluffy world for a couple hours and came out smelling of lemons and roses with wonderfully painted toes. I then decided that it was very important to have good eyebrows for my birthday. As I still have eyebrows I may as well make them good ones, so my second birthday treat was decided, eyebrow threading it was.

With perfectly shaped eyebrows and wonderfully painted toes I had dinner with 2 lovely boys, Peter and Calvin at The Cheshire Cat. Perfect! I actually managed to stay out after dinner to listen to some live music. It must have been the eyebrows and toes that gave me extra energy, whatever it was I had a glorious time. I left like a small child, full of excitement at having such a good evening.

So, I am now worn out and will probably have to sleep for a couple of days to get over my day, but it was so worth   it. Days like today are my golden glimmers, the clear sky I can see through the clearing mist. These days are real life and utterly glorious.

My rock and roll today has been full of beans and clearing mist, I've loved it.

15th August 2013

It was all going so well. I have however, learnt not to get too comfortable in the 'all is well' frame of mind as something always seems to come and remind me that maybe all is not altogether well. I have had two little reminders today that I wasn't expecting. I used to love surprises, I can say with all honesty I am going off them fairly rapidly as none of my surprises have been of the nice variety.

So first thing this morning whilst handing Miss Daisy back to me, Dave, my ex decided to tell me that he is now with someone else. I of course knew all along but he had denied it all this time and chose today to come clean. I am happy for him and all that, I really am and that is not me protesting too much, it just takes it all to another level and I hadn't expected that to happen today.

No time like the present I guess. It will take miss picky pants here a little longer to reciprocate that kind of admission,

I don't thing chemotherapy and life changing nonsense like this is conducive for dating. Shocker!

Anyway, the second thing today was a visit to the   oncologist. Not Mr. Blinky Eyes. This one was the oncologist who dealt with the radiotherapy, or so I thought. I have been trying to cancel this appointment as it seemed utterly pointless in the light of having cancer again and chemotherapy. I naively thought they would know this when

I got there and NO – they knew nothing.

I had to explain everything, and I mean everything. I had never seen this oncologist before and I was getting really cross that he knew nothing about me or why I was even there. There must also be a rule at Oncology school that once an Oncologist has qualified they must never make eye contact with the patient. This guy had his eyes closed. No kidding. This made me crosser.

So, I wonder how many consultants one girl needs whilst having cancer, it seems I have 3. All of them with slightly different views of the world. Luckily I know my stuff about my cancer and was having none of what he was saying, dare I say I may have scared Mr. Shut Eyes a little with my exasperation of the situation and the cheek of him trying

to suggest things when he clearly knew nothing about me and what the plan was. At the end of the appointment he asked me if I wanted to see him again. When I asked why I would want to when I have 2 other consultants who are doing everything for me and know me and my situation and surely that's enough, he actually couldn't answer me. In fact, he couldn't answer any question I asked.

I wont be seeing him again. The bit I hadn't bargained for however, was a check up. Of course that was always going to happen, but as I couldn't work out why I was there in the first place I hadn't prepared myself for this. I was no longer cross, I was terrified. This was the first check up since I had found the second lump. I, naked from the waist up as usual in these circumstances, lay crying on the bed absolutely terrified that he was going to find something.

I explained this to him. His retort was, don't worry it's usually one in a thousand that we find something - Oh. I was unlucky then finding 2 in 5 months - the room went quiet and Mr. Shut Eyes was speechless.

At least it stopped him talking nonsense to me.   So, no lumps or bumps to be found. Phew! My throat allowed me to breath again and my heart stopped racing and I found my head enough to get cross when Mr. Shut Eyes

started again about treatment that was completely inappropriate for me.

And even more inappropriate that he's not even my consultant. At this point Mr. Blinky Eyes seemed like a dream doctor. I'll stick with him.

Luckily the gorgeous Gaby was on hand and we concluded that these meetings are always going to make me feel terrified, association of bad news and all that. This one was silly and unnecessary and I should have gone with my instincts of not going to it. I will know next time to stick to Mr. Blinky Eyes and Mr. Cautious Surgeon.

So, tired out as I predicted from my glorious day yesterday, I have spent the day fire fighting a little but with the loveliness of Gorgeous Gaby to remind me that it aint all bad.

A quite confused rock and roll today, but rock and roll all the same. I am sure a normal service will resume tomorrow, it better as it's my birthday in 2 days and I don't want to be singing 'it's my party and I'll cry if I want to'!

16th August 2013

I've got that birthday feeling bubbling up inside. I get as excited about my birthday now as I did when I had jelly and ice cream at my parties and

I'm not talking vodka jellies, I'm talking the kind of jelly and ice cream Miss Daisy likes to throw around. I'm super exited as tomorrow I get to wear high heals and go out with my super girlie girls.

I have not worn high heals since I have been ill the second time around. That's 3 months of no high heal wearing. That's far too long for this girl, chemo or no chemo, my high heels are coming out to play tomorrow and I can't wait!

So today it feels like I have been on holiday. Gin Jayne picked me and Miss Daisy up and took us to Wales to a park with a river that the kids played in. The sun was shining and we all had a mild holiday feeling going on. It's always a good day out with gin Jayne where ever we go and today was no exception, of course we swapped gin for coffee and water for our picnic but I am sure we can make up for that tomorrow, not that chemo birthday girl here can drink very much but I am so looking forward to a glass of something, I know for sure that one wont hurt.

So, birthday plans are sorted. Miss Daisy has told me that she is going to wake me up and sing happy birthday to me and then I can make pancakes for us both. I have presents that are all wrapped up that I have had all on stopping Miss Daisy from opening, or telling me what they are. Me and Miss Daisy are going out for lunch with Dave and then I am leaving her with him and coming home to get myself ready for my high heel wearing night out. We are of course going out super early just in case I get too tired and need to come home. That is not to do with my age! With my super regenerated body, I must now be younger than when I started chemo, so who knows how old I really am.

So my rock and roll is full of birthday excitement, high heels, super girlie girls and I can't wait!

17th August 2013

The sign of a good birthday.   Not remembering coming home! It is not normal to enjoy a hangover, but today, it is the best feeling ever.

So, it was my birthday, I decided that I was 34 which worked for everyone, especially me. It was also the day me and Miss Daisy should have been going on holiday to Spain to meet with my beautiful Nessa, but clearly that wasn't going to happen due to all this nonsense, but we didn't let that get us down. I did instead bask in the warmth of my friends very amazing glow.

So, it started with a phone call from Abby, a great way to start birthday proceedings. Miss Daisy then woke up, yes I was awake before her, I said I got excited didn't I, and she sang happy birthday and then she opened my presents. A BOSE iPod dock thing was in the box. It seemed the right thing to do was to try it out, so early doors me and Miss Daisy were dancing and singing in the kitchen.

We have the same favourite songs, Madonna's 'Holiday' and Helen Reddy's 'I am Woman' She knows the words to both and we have some cool moves, but of course I would say that and remember no one is watching or listening and that is probably best! Helen Reddys song has sort of got me through some tricky days and I am a little concerned I won't be able to listen to it after all this, it makes me feel invincible and sometimes I need to feel like that when faced with the fear.

So, we then went out for lunch with Dave and that's where I left Miss Daisy to come home and get myself ready for my first night out in absolutely months. Plan B kept me company, another perfect way to spend a birthday, and I sang and danced my way to getting out of the house for 6pm. We started early as I was concerned I wouldn't be awake long enough. There was no need to worry. It seemed I was on form on the drinking and staying awake front which completely took me by surprise, in a good way. I had the best reminder a girl needs that friends are by far the best things any one could have and I have the best, by a country mile.

So, my birthday rock and roll was full of friends and lots and lots of love, oh and a mojito, a real life one! I had a ball!

ps. Tomorrow is birthday picnic time, I can't remember where or when but I am sure someone will tell me!

18th August 2013

Sunshine, fresh air and mischief is where it's been at

today. So, some occasions just need celebrating, whatever is going on in the world, and this year my birthday was one of them. I have made it this far in a relatively sane fashion through all this nonsense and I'm in one of my good weeks, what's not to celebrate! And last night we were all in the same cheeky frame of mind and we all fancied a   celebratory tipple, it would have been rude not to. It was a much needed very funny night out with some very funny girls that made me laugh all night. We have all been feeling a little fragile today but I have strangely enjoyed it as it was worth every inch of my delicateness.

Today the sun was shining and we all headed for Attingham Park with our children and slightly sore heads with promises that the fresh air would blow away the cob webs. I have had a sense of mischief with me all day and it seemed that the gorgeous Gaby, master baker Catriona and the lovely Christine were all just as kiddy as me. It is fair to say we spent the afternoon laughing at more or less   anything. Perfect! It was in fact the perfect end to my birthday weekend. I was spoilt rotten with flowers, amazing gifts and much much laughing, just what this girl needed. Oh and I got to twirl and spin with Miss Daisy, with nobody watching, of course, I hope anyway!

I am now however resorting to bribery with Miss Daisy to come to bed with me early so I can get some much needed sleep, my throat feels like its sore and I can't afford to get ill now as treatment no. four is on Thursday. And the only thing worse than treatment is not having it on time. I have had my super green drink and all my other concoctions to get me back to fighting fit

again which will happen in no time, in fact I can feel it working already.
On the count down to treatment day I think I should be able to fly like
super woman with the amount of goodness my body gets, all in the name
of getting through that day as best I can.

The strange memory thing has happened already as I can't remember
how bad the cold cap was last time, or the treatment itself, phew! This
clever selective memory thing may just get me to the end of this treatment
with hair as long as it decides to stay with me that is. We decided
yesterday we were very proud of my hair for hanging around. That's
possibly an understatement, I'm blooming ecstatic!

So my rock and roll has been full of mischief and laughing and long may
it continue.

19th August 2013

So, the pre treatment fear starts to creep in around about now. It's a
bugger really as all can be fine in my world and then I remember what I
will be doing on Thursday and I get jittery and mildly uncomfortable with
the whole idea.

All day today I have been doing my best to bargain with time and see if I
can speed it up in my head to get me through the next few days. These
few days will of course be filled with cleaning and tidying and sorting out
and generally getting me ready for time out of action. The day itself is
sorted which is the biggest relief as I need the calm and order that is
experience of what happens, its far too freaky otherwise.

It's not all dull and uninteresting as I am meeting my 2 boss's tomorrow which I am looking forward to and I have the next 3 days with Miss Daisy and she loves to clean and tidy. Not. I am sure we will squeeze in some frivolity along the way.

It's not helping that I am feeling utterly exhausted today, my pay back from having such a good birthday no doubt, I can live with that as long as I remember that is what it is and not some horrible emotional dip. It can be easily confused in my current state of emotional rollercoasterness that goes hand in hand with all this nonsense, at least I am wise enough to know when this is a trick one - completely out of being too tired. A super early night is required to get this girl back on form.

Rachel said that this nonsense is possibly harder to deal   with emotionally rather than physically and boy is she right. I have never in my life been in such an emotional state of the good, bad, absolutely terrified

to completely enlightened and all that can happen in the same day sometimes, no wonder I'm so tired! This is not in an insane, oh my god she's lost the plot way reminiscent of breakdownsville times, they are very rational and logical but, occasionally very emotional   times.

But even through all of that I have still laughed an awful lot. I believe that really is down to those who are by my side, near and far, who pick me up when I fall and make me giggle the rest of the time. Oh and I think I may be slightly determined myself to get through some of the pickles, no fake smiling allowed in my world.

So my bribery yesterday worked with Miss Daisy and we both went to bed at the same time, crazy cat that I am! I believe the same will be happening tonight. Somebody stop me, again! I have loaded myself up with vegetables, vitamins, and all manor of goodness and it's time to let sleep work its magic.

So, my very exciting rock and roll is full of keeping my emotions at bay, managing the fear and letting the magic happen when I hit the sheets. Crazy!

20th August 2013

So, I have kept the fear at bay today by occupying my mind with all things work. I have, of course, been with the MAB massive that is Robin and James.

I could pretend that I was in the real world for a couple of hours which got me very excited as I could feel the glimmer of gold that is the end of all this nonsense and the start of my real life again.

So I got to catch up with the working world, which I have missed. And I got flowers which was a real treat – garage bought or not, the thought I think was there. Apparently I look too well, mmm, surely that should be a good thing but it also fair to say that looks can be very deceiving. Typical male perspective. They should try seeing me in a couple of days time, that may change their view. I'm not criticizing – work have been truly amazing.

Anyway, I may be allowed to do some bits and bobs of work at home if my brain returns to some sort of normality after this next cycle. That is if I can convince the MAB massive that I am ok, which I sure hope I can if I am.

Una from The Saturdays says that after cycle four some people's brain power comes back, that would be very nice if mine decided to come home. I have so missed being able to do more than just look at pictures in magazines and watch absolutely crap TV. Honestly, I think I have probably watched all of Friends again, although recently I have ventured into such treats as Columbo and Magnum PI. That is how little of my brain occupies my head however good a young Tom Selleck looks

So, all excited about the thought of work and actually being able to think about it without my head becoming full of fog, I get Miss Daisy and we head home. Amelia and Lucy get the big clean and Miss daisy decides to turn the slide into a water slide and she spends most of the afternoon soaking wet. I get to give the house it's very own big clean ready for my out of action days looming and all is well with the world.

A big treat. My heart filled with magical joy as X Factor was advertised to start very soon, not only that but all the autumn drama type programmes are all being advertised. I know we are still in the throws of summer and in normal circumstances the world does not revolve around TV, but in a chemotherapy fuelled world it unfortunately does. When my chemo started I said that when its over, Simon Cowell's and his clan will be back. My time is not far away. This was a big moment.

So, tomorrow, early doors I am having my blood taken to see if I'm OK for treatment number four on Thursday. Let's hope I am or there will be trouble, we can't be straying from this very tight schedule of mine. I have done everything I can to be fighting fit, so fingers crossed my body has done what it needs to be ready to start this all over again.

So, today my rock and roll has been full of the excitement of work, more glimmers of gold, and the heart warming joy of Gary Barlow in my living room.

<u>21st August 2013</u>

So, we are on for treatment number 4 in the morning. I am very proud of my body; you know that it has done it's stuff ready to go through it all again. And although I am happy each treatment is happening to plan so far, I am filled with the fear all over again about what I have to do tomorrow. It's a very strange feeling as I have absolutely no choice about what is coming and I know it's really magic in disguise but all the same, it's horrible, and it's a blooming good disguise.

Anyway, early doors I had a new nurse come and take my blood. Pauline George, we now affectionately call her Georgie Fame, yes I know she is a she, but at the risk of not finding a good music name for her, Georgie Fame is good enough. So, Georgie Fame was lovely, as all the nurses are. She was very impressed with my hair, as in the amount left, and that's always a good start! Daisy became Georgie Fames helper and was very into the whole taking of the blood and blood pressure, she even signed my name at the end for me which was rather impressive but no doubt very dangerous for the future.

Georgie Fame's best words of the day were to say that treatment no.four means getting over the hump, it feels like it will be quicker when tomorrow is done. Music to my ears. six weeks tomorrow and I will be having my last visit from Ms. Saturdays needles. Hallelujah!

Georgie Fame had some very good advice on how I can get through the next three treatments which calmed me down a lot. It involved pain killers and mild sedation to chill me out enough to handle the cold cap and treatment. The morning of treatment is very testing for me, it takes me everything I have to do it and that causes all sorts of emotional and physical feelings. Last time I felt so sick and that was before any drugs were in me. Georgie Fame puts this down to nerves and tension. Take that away a little and all could be better. I will give anything a go through this so bring on the sedation!

Luckily I have 3 magic pills left from diagnosis days and with three treatments left clearly its meant to be. So I have everything crossed that it just takes the edge off enough to get through the day without too much drama. Of course I also have the gorgeous Gaby here for the day to get me through, along with Una from The Saturdays so all should be as good as it can be when this nonsense is involved.

So, swinging was the rest of my day. And by swinging I don't mean the swapping of partner's kind, really not my thing. I, of course mean the swinging on swings in the park kind. Miss Daisy actually learnt how to swing on her own today which our achievement, and boy was it a good one. It finally clicked with her and once she got it there was no stopping her. So Miss Daisy and me spent hours on the swings, perfect!

So, my rock and roll has been full of sedation, swinging and fighting the fear, safe in the knowledge this time tomorrow I will be another one down, two thirds done with six weeks to go.

<u>23rd August 2013</u>

Well, treatment number 4 over and out, with cold cap   on, whoop whoop! I am very, very proud of myself for getting though yesterday in such a calm manner.

Lots of things contributed.

 Knowing I was in the very good hands of the gorgeous Gaby and Una from The Saturdays. A little routine has developed and yesterday it worked a treat. We made a few tweaks on the cold cap front which made it more comfortable, to the point that me and the gorgeous Gaby missed the time it was to come off as we chatted, watched a movie and she rubbed my feet through it. How bizarre! And not let's forget I could have rattled with the amount of drugs I'd had before it all kicked off! But boy did they make a difference, Georgie Fame was sure right, thank goodness she came across my path when she did, she may just have saved my hair!

So, I am feeling super sick now and very tired with a banging headache, but with no scalp burn on this occasion which feels a bit better already.

My plans for today are the same as last night, move as little as possible and try and sleep as much as I can. Such a crazy start to the bank holiday weekend. As soon as this magic in disguise has worked it's real magic in my body it needs to get the hell out and leave me to myself again. Not long now.

That's all I got right now.

My rock and roll is full of the mild sickly, knackered excitement that I'm over the hump, four down and two to go and in less than six weeks I'll be done with this part of the nonsense. That's pretty good rock and roll when I'm feeling this bad.

24th August 2013

So, I made it past number four relatively successfully and am feeling tired and sick but not too bad. Something has been slightly different this time as I have an optimism that I haven't had since this has started and that is because I can actually see the finish line. I was lying awake last night with my mind working over time. I also watched two films from start to finish in bed which I have not been able to do at this early stage in the game.

The lovely Christine came for her regular Friday after treatment visit which is always good and keeps me sane. I'm really rubbish company but she comes and talks to me about I can't really remember what, but it is just what I need.

I then managed to sleep, eat and sleep some more in between having all my meds. The down side of sleeping so much in the day, which I can't stop as I can't actually keep my eyes open, is I am awake in the night.

Alex Jagger

Last night I could not stop my mind from going crazy. Two things   were whirling around.

The first thing is someone said to me last week that what I write in this blog is very open and personal to my whole   life. I asked at the time if that was wrong or right. I'm not sure I remembered the response, it was a good response whatever it was. I have given this much thought. Last night I had it straight in my head. Having cancer has effected every inch of my life and the lives of those around me to a point. It also has the severe side effect of depression, that is well documented but I also can say that from my experience of my first diagnosis, you know the heading to breakdownsville and not dealing with anything very well. I was like a ten armed animal not knowing what to do, how to be and being really scared all the time. I didn't want to talk about anything to do with having cancer as I thought I had it nailed.

But those very big decisions to be made by me about me were the things that freaked me right out. I lost all sense of being Alex Jagger and that's no good for anybody, especially me. The thing that pulled me right out of it, finding a second lump and thinking I could die of this god awful disease.

That, in normal circumstances should have taken me deeper into depression and despair, but it didn't, it made me fight for my own survival. And I started to write down how I felt. I am clearly better at writing it down than talking about it, who cares as long as its out.

So the answer to that first question is I am doing it for very selfish reasons. For my own sanity and to sort through what's in my head at the time so it doesn't stay there and take me back to a place I can't be. I teeter on the edge of reason most days but get myself out of any dark places by writing this   and remembering who I have around me. And in my head on any given day could be just about anything, hence the whole life experience I am sharing.

The second point whirling around follows on from the first point. Someone, many months ago very   randomly enlightened me on my Chinese sign and element. I was born in the year of the dog and I am metal. So, the dog bit first. I am fiercely loyal to my friends, those I love and those I work for, I always have been and I always will be,   I don't think that's new news. I have, however, a very selfish streak with others that probably dates back to abandonment issues from my teenage years when my mum died and the rest of my family buggered off. I believe its called self preservation.

I actually, mistakenly misplaced my self preservation in my breakdownsville stage and it's not quite come back yet.

Life is a little too vulnerable without it. What was new news however, was the metal part. I had never seen that in me until now.

So, metal. I need to stop giving myself a hard time. My favourite past time. I lay in bed last night and realised what I am doing and what I have done.

My heart has been broken by life, by cancer and by the struggle that is chemotherapy and the fear that is facing up to one's own mortality twice.

The good bits, however, are the putting all of this back together in a way that fits and is happy and healthy.

I am very determined not to come out of this depressed by the shock of what has been. I read a lot yesterday on other people's blogs - reading, ha! - and they all said how depressed they are now it's over and the tail spin they find themselves in of not dealing with it whilst it was happening and realising the severity of it once it was over.

I am not going to be that girl. I have cried a million tears since December last year when all this started, I have gone to the depths of my despair more times than I care to talk about and I have faced up to some real life challenges and I have lived with a constant pain inside me for nearly nine months.

The best bit of all this, I can see a way out, the light at the end of the tunnel, a clear path in front on me once this is over because I am dealing with it through writing it down and bearing my soul to anyone or no one, that doesn't matter, as long as it's out. I am made of tough stuff I decided in the early hours of this morning! Possibly metal.

So, this change on cycle number four is quite enlightening for me. It was the fact that I have being having chemo for three months and I have less than six weeks left.

What takes six weeks?

The school summer holidays which I bet everyone is saying now how they have flown by; my radiotherapy took six weeks. That's a bad example as that felt like a lifetime through the worse of my breakdownsville time. I said ages ago that when Miss Daisy goes back to school it may feel like it's not far away, that's a week on Tuesday. I know I am the master at bargaining with time, but it has done me well so far!

So it seems I am full of tired but optimistic rock and roll today, full of the reasons of why I am sharing quite so   much. You have no idea how it's helping me not be that girl at the end of this. Remember, I am determined to smile and mean it.

25th August 2013

Patience and the ability to listen, not my best qualities in previous times. They are, however, becoming two things I have had little choice but to get my head around, very reluctantly I might add. I will start with the ability to   listen.

This is one thing that may have frustrated most people I know, mainly as when I make my mind up about something I tend not to listen to anyone else and just go for it. Not a bad thing I always said, but I would wouldn't I. Of course I will listen to my friends till the cows come home about practically anything but I am of course talking, on this occasion, about listening to my body. Another thing I have never been able to do, until now.

As I was precariously propped up on the sofa by   cushions yesterday unable to move very much due to severe lack of anything that resembled energy, I realised that I have actually been very good at listening to my body through all of this and have done exactly what it has told me.

Now that   is unusual! It may be possibly the reason why I have got through each cycle well, as I'm doing what I'm told, for a change.

The other. Patience. Really not my strong point. I think that may have come across with the bargaining with time debacle that goes on daily in my head and in my writing.

I am always told at work to be more considered, less impatient. But again once I make my mind up I go like a rocket, again not bad I always thought, as long as the decision was the right one! I always thought it was - but I would.

However, I may have just come some way without really realising it.

This   again occurred to me yesterday whilst unable to do very much when I realised that I haven't done too bad on this front. Three months. That's how much chemo I have done to date, not bad I say. I have listened to everyone and taken everyone's advice, I have researched the hell out of   this nonsense to get through it the best way for me. I have been considered and taken time, I believe that's called listening with some patience! Who'd have thought it was possible.

So, yesterday came and went, which is just how I wanted it to go. I had a lovely visit from gorgeous Kate from next   door. She came bearing birthday gifts, always a good start, and also great bargaining with time chat, which I love, with some patience of course.

We worked out that I have less than six weeks left and the way it's going at the moment I am completely out of action for probably four days

after each treatment. So with two cycles left, lets call it a   week. So, in six weeks I have one week out of action and five weeks with not much energy or brain power, but still not sick   or debilitated and able to go out and do stuff. And there are loads of stuff in the diary that are all treatment and surgery related.

She also pointed out that as soon as I get my surgery meeting done it will give me a whole new focus. Clever   Kate!   She is of course right. Surgery is different and does not phase me in the slightest. Yes, it will be painful and there will be recovery involved but it does not mess with my head the same way chemotherapy does. There will be no fog, no lack of energy, no lack of brain power, no constant nausea one week out of three, no cold cap and no toxic drugs just glorious, fear free new boobs courtesy of Dan the Boob Man and his fellow surgeons. And then it's all done, time for the rest of my life to begin.

Actually I think that is sort of happening around me, you know, the rest of my life, in a whole new, improved way but still very much made up of all things Alex Jagger.

I am hoping today passes quite as well as yesterday did as I'm still as knackered. Miss Daisy is home tomorrow, I have missed her so very much but it's right she doesn't see her very boring not being able to move very much mummy over these past few days, mainly as she would be bored stupid.

I need to remember that when I am trying to teach Miss Daisy about patience and listening, that she is very like me, lets see how that works out for us.

So, my rock and roll today will be filled with fluffy cushions mainly propping me up. That works for me.

26th August 2013

So, I listened to my body very well yesterday. And it seemed all it talked about was food. Of the Sunday roast variety to be specific. Bizarre that 3 days in I am craving a Sunday Roast. This is the girl who was being propped up by cushions and sleeping, not cooking a Sunday Roast. But, I could not ignore the shouts and screams for Yorkshire puddings, roast potatoes and gravy. And yes it is very clear that I am a true Yorkshire girl. There is no escaping that.

So, I dragged myself up, put myself in the shower and got myself into my car, dressed of course and drove to the shops to get all the component parts to create my craving and got myself home and cooked. That in itself is a miracle, chemo or no chemo, cooking a Sunday roast for me comes around about once a year. But I did a fairly good job and ate the lot. If it was possible to be drunk on food, I was hammered.

So waking up with a slight food hangover, I got ready for the return of Miss Daisy and a trip to Attingham Park. I am aiming to walk every day once out of the woods as I am sure it helps my body and soul. And my soul was more on my mind than my body today as I felt peculiar from the minute I woke up. That really is nothing new as every day I have some sort of enlightened moment, exhausting really, but this was a little different to the usual. Maybe because I am getting closer to the end of this hardest bit that I am daring to test the waters of the future. And that coupled with the fact I always feel odd for the first few days after my toxic abuse. Today I felt at odds with the world, as if uneasy about something like something was going to happen that maybe   I wasn't going to like.

I realised that maybe it's those pesky little lightning bolt jolts of reality that remind me of what has been happening. I think a lot, too much some would say, and I know I think far too much in the first few days after my treatment as generally I can't do anything else. I also think I made the mistake of getting carried away with the fact I could actually read something and read someone else's blog about how depressed they were, must not do that again.

So, today whilst walking with the lovely Christine in the too hot sun for my super sensitive skin I resolved to not be that girl. You know the one that is scared that the sky is going to fall in.

No. I'm not doing that. Instead I am putting a date in my diary for some sort of celebration for the end of   my chemotherapy and another one for the end of my surgery and then we're done. I am not going to finish this only to fall into some deep hole. Been there, done that and not going back. I deserve a medal not a therapy session.

So with this revelation put to the back of my mind, I focused on the only thing I could and that was food. Again. Steak this time. I have an appetite that has come out of nowhere, always the same in these few days so may as well enjoy it.

Random really, as soon as I stop feeling sick I can't stop eating. Making up for lost time no doubt. So off for steak me and Miss Daisy went.

So my rock and roll today has been full of walking, sunshine, not letting the sky fall in and steak. Not bad for day four of no. four.

27th August 2013

Feet saved me today. Of the wonderfully massaged kind that is. My day has all been a little odd. I am putting it down to the toxic poisoning and my very annoying mind that will not give it a rest. Today I have been very tired and strangely so has Miss Daisy.

We spent most of our day together watching films in our PJ's which was divine, but my mind was not allowing me to enjoy the moment quite as much as I would have hoped. Tired unsettledness kept getting in the way.

So, in five weeks' time I will be about to have my last treatment, I think that is why I feel at odds with everything. It feels close, sometimes very close and maybe I am getting a little excited about the prospect but dare not as it is still five weeks away. And five weeks is still five weeks however I try and spin it. Part of me wants to run to the hill tops and shout very loud that I am nearly at the end of this horribleness and part of me thinks I should be reserved and wait it out.

It's all Just Rock n' Roll

Luckily I am not of the reserved disposition and also luckily I am not about to run anywhere as I may end up in a collapsed sorry heap of exhaustion. So there lies the source of my confusion, I have no idea how to be, in me or in my head. I guess on the plus side someone must have put lead in my body in the night as I am so ridiculously tired I will no doubt be sleeping through most of my unsettledness this week which is no bad thing. I have been told from the start that chemotherapy effects everyone slightly differently but one sure thing is tiredness. And to be fair I am still only in the first week after my treatment so maybe I should give myself a break.

So, I do the Miss Daisy drop off and head off for all things reflexology, against my will I have to say.

I had the fear a little, the fear of just bursting into tears at the first spoken word or the fear of not being able to stop my mind from doing the loop the loop whilst there. To help all this nonsense I decide to park afar and walk in, you know my daily walk. That helped. And it seemed I had no need to worry as I was truly saved by Miss Mary's magic hands on my feet. An hour of savior time and I left with a spring in my step, not a tear or loop the loop in site.

Back to what's important and I got fish and chips on the way home from the best fish shop in the world, around the corner from my house. I am clearly trying to eat all the nations favourite dishes in one week, if I have a curry tomorrow I think I will be about there.

So, my rock and roll is of the super tired variety with a little unsettled confusion thrown in for good measure.

Alex Jagger

BMX bikes and feeling touched by nice people has been my day, with a whole lot of tiredness and food thrown in for very good measure. I won't go on about food, although I am well aware I have for a few days now, mainly as I astound myself at the amount I eat so soon after such toxic poisoning. It does calm down or I really would be the size of a small house.

It just amazes me what my body is doing. I can also see that this really just amazes me (no one else), so I will move on.

So, the really big news today was that Miss Daisy learnt to ride a bike without stabilisers. Today I was that mum in the park shrieking with excitement as Dave ran along side her as she rode solo for the first time. I was of course left behind on account of not being able to move quit as fast, as once she started she just did not stop! You'd have thought today that no one had ever ridden a bike ever before the way I was going on, but hey, you only get one shot at these first times. She's a determined little monkey and as her reward for cracking this particular nut she got her very first proper bike, you know one without stabilisers. A BMX of course. She's such a cool dude. But of course I would say that.

So, with Miss Daisy beyond excited at her achievement and new bike and me beyond excited at her cracking it I got the chance to stop and think about how nice people   are.

Random. Possibly. But never has there been a time in my life that I have realised how nice people are. That sounds really obvious under these sort of circumstances to me, although I can't imagine how I will express my utter everything to those that have got me through once this is over. I am sure I will find a way when It's right but it sort of over whelms me a little right now.

And I have to stop using the word nice, my mum used to say it was a very common word and I should try and use a more expressive one! So in light of that, I'll say touching instead.

Sometimes, something happens that takes me by surprise. Of the good kind. And today has been a lovely reminder of how I am in people's minds without me even realising it. It was really down to some miso soup, an email from work and a whatsapp message. I have ridiculously sore veins, so sore you can see the bruises on the outside that are inside. Miss Daisy thinks they are bones in my arms they are so taught. Nice. Not. really. I have read that miso soup and gallons of water help. The gallons of water are easy, but I have been unable to find miso soup. Not sure if it's my lack of brain or I just can't find any. Today Dave turned up with some for me and I can't even remember telling him about it, but he had seen how bad my veins were and had managed to find some,

Secondly, Robin, part of the MAB massive, touched me incredibly with his kind words that he broadcast to the world that really took me by surprise and made me feel incredibly lucky all at the same time and thirdly a message from someone I've worked with for years but not heard from, completely out of the blue just checking to see how I was.

All sounds very simple really with all this going on, but just sometimes things other than the usual make me stop and think for all the right reasons.

So I felt all warm and fluffy from the inside out, which makes a good change from the usual confused turmoil that seems to be on a constant loop. Although the confused turmoil is not always so confused and it isn't always turmoil, but you know what I mean.

So, my rock and roll has been full of cycling Miss Daisy's and feeling warm and fluffy, not an ounce of confusion in sight.

29th August 2013

It all started so well today, I was still on my fluffy high from yesterday and apart from a minor div moment this morning all was going to plan. Miss Daisy returned home and was more excited to see her BMX bike than me but we had all things girls planned so I let that bit go. The order of the day was agreed and we were about to start off when I had a phone call from the estate agents, someone wanted to view the house today, it only went on the marketing this morning, a good start I thought. Of course the house was a mess, the double act that is Miss Daisy and me managed to transform it miraculously into a dream home someone would of course want to buy.

Polish and mops put aside and the day continued, starting at the hairdressers for Daisy. I decided that I am channeling my lack of hair through my daughter's beautiful hair which seemed to work for both of us.

The rest of the day went great and we had a girlie ball made up of whipped cream hot chocolate, nails, photos and the boring bit, school uniform shopping. Just as we were heading home the people viewing the house cancelled. Bugger. They don't like the train station. Never mind, some one will. I don't live in a train station by the way, just quite close to one, which I think is great.

Anyway, I then decide I had to sort the house out a bit more and had a rush of organisational type behaviour going on that Miss Daisy decided she wanted to get in on and whilst she cleaned out the fish tank I got things done that have needed to be done for months. I then had to clean up the mess from the fish tank as that was a mistake! Poor fish.

So I get to late evening and started to feel mighty odd, and I realised I had not eaten anything all day. What a difference a day makes! I soon sorted that out.

So I braved some crap TV and whilst channel flicking the big build comes on and low and behold its a family effected by cancer. At this point normally I frantically turn over or run out of the room with my hands over my ears, randomly. For the first time I watched and listened. I watched a man who has had cancer talk about his prognosis.

Turns out it's the same as mine. Get to 5 years and all is very good, get to 10 years and it looks like your cured. I am very up beat about that bit as it means I am alive. This poor chap

was so depressed and down and had a 'whatever' type of tone in his voice. I think that's the fear that stays with some people and the untrusting nature of this disease. Luckily I think I am doing a good job at exorcising those demons to make sure they don't live me when its time for all this nonsense to be put behind me. I hope the poor chap on TV manages to do the same.

So although my day started well, had a dip of enthusiasm and a random lack of energy I managed to emotionally keep   it together when I would normally wobble. That TV programme made me realise that I am not doing too bad at all, in my head and in my body. She says absolutely knackered!

So my rock and roll today has been all about Miss Daisy and keeping my emotions in check just for a change.

30th August 2013

August needs to end, soon. It has been the longest month in the history of longest months. For me that is. I can feel my energy dwindling along with my good frame of mind   today which is not part of my plan, but then again it never is.

The almighty headache that really likes hanging out with me cannot be helping how I am getting through the day, I think I

always get these about now, just part of this ridiculous situation I find myself in and today I can't see the end of it, how ever hard I have tried.

So, trying to get myself out of this dark place I go to see a house with Miss Daisy, of course I haven't sold the one I am in but it doesn't stop me seeing what's out there I guess and as this was new it was just a show home. I'm drawn to low maintenance no nonsense living after all this as there is no way, once all this is over, I'm spending my weekends doing a house up, I've done enough painting thank you very   much.

Then off to Attingham Park which was lovely to catch up with the birthday afternoon tea girls as it distracted me more than enough for the afternoon. Miss Daisy found a climbing wall and got herself to the top, she was very pleased with herself.

So, what happened to my head after such a nice afternoon only I guess my head can answer and some times me and my head are not on the same wave length. A whole wave of sadness covered me, that's what happened.

I have had some lovely messages from work this week and one today, again, made me realise how shocked some people have been about me.

And, although it's lovely people care, it shocks me again too. And it is still bloody August! Plus, I also have had new

thoughts today that I haven't had before. Quite bizarre really and I'm actually not going to go into them right now as I'm not sure I have it straight in my own head yet but it relates to my type of major surgery and being single. Random. Very possibly.

I have realised that my coping mechanism allows me only to think about things in small, bite sized chunks. Too much in one go and I will be in a whole new place of self discovery that involves white walls and not much else. Something in my head must have thought I was ready to take on the next phase in this utter ridiculous nonsense. The surgery bit doesn't scare me like the chemo did but it does take some thinking about.

Thinking about what is actually being done to me to be specific. Again I don't have a choice and even if I did I would be doing the same but suddenly I am very aware that quite a significant part of me will be very different very soon. Fear free. That's all I have to remember. On the plus side, I am getting close to seeing those surgeons again which can only mean one thing. Chemo is nearly done. Every cloud and all that.

On white walls, I had a dream last night that my house was completely white and

I couldn't distinguish anything as everything was, well, white. Maybe I have already gone mad.

So, my rock and roll today has a very sore head from the inside out. This girl needs to sleep. Tomorrow is a new day.

<u>31st August 2013</u>

Hurray for the last day of August! September looks so very inviting. Surely it has to be better than its close friends May, June, July and August. And surely it has to be in a different league to its acquaintances December, January, February, March and April Lets hope so or I may have to write a letter of complaint. I am holding out for September,

October and November to restore my faith in the months of the year. If something good doesn't happen in these three, then I'm sending them all back and demanding a full refund.

Anyway, yesterday I was walking through mud, or that's how it felt and feels getting through this at times. Today, being a new dawn and a new day and all that I started this new day cross with my dreams. They can be so cruel at times and last night was a little reminder of that I do not have.

So I did the only thing I could think of and baked some banana bread. As you do. Miss Daisy's favourite breakfast is my banana bread so when she woke up this morning she had that freshly made treat waiting for her. Her smile is very contagious so that worked for both of us.

I am not one for self pity, in general, but I do know   that sometimes it's necessary and it happens. But I also know that

it really isn't good for the soul. Last night I really felt sorry for myself. Last night all I could see was the same situation stretching out in front of me and last night   I wasn't actually sure how I was going to make it through with my sanity.

At times I look at where I am now and wonder how on earth I made it so far and I'm a little scared that my 'being able to get through' stuff that's within me may be running out of steam. Today I am still a little daunted by my heavy heart but the dawning of a new month is giving me something, who knows what, but something. And most of the time something is better than nothing.

So, here endeth my session of self pity, I've decided it's not a good look and really does not suit me. I'm a massive fan of winter boots, mainly of the high heeled variety, and as all the new season boots are now making an appearance it's time for my new season to make an appearance too, in boots preferably. I am so wishing away the end of my flip flop wearing summer that to me has lasted about a year. I believe I am bargaining with time once more. Why change the daily habit of a very unfortunate year's lifetime.

So, today I get to catch up with some of my favourite people who have been on holiday.

As they are probably hitting the post holiday blues I am super

happy that they are back! (Sorry!) Miss Daisy gets to party hard at her favourite type of party, a princess one of course and I can't let today go by without mentioning the start of X Factor!

This is not because it's my favourite programme, it is of course because when my chemotherapy started I stated that by the time I finished it, X Factor would be on TV. That day has come, hurray!

And in thirty three days' time I will be having my last treatment. I'm getting there.

So, my rock and roll today is full of favourite people, parties and the appearance of Gary Barlow on my sofa. Oh and new season boots.

<u>1st September 2013</u>

The first day of September, ah, how I have longed for this month to begin. The first day of a new season of seasons, the first day of thirty two left of my treatment and of course the first day of a new season of boots! As I turned the page of my calendar on the fridge this morning I had the joy, if that is the right word, to see both my last treatments on the same page. Not long now.

Many people have many different experiences of chemotherapy, which of course makes sense as we are all very different. People have told me that the last treatment

was by far the worse, some the middle one, some the fourth one, some the first. I think anyone can discount the first as that is full of terror so will never be comparable to anything. So, of course I have given this much thought. (Shocker!) I have decided that they are going to be as good or as bad as they are going to be. The last one quite frankly can do what it needs to do as I won't be doing it again, ever.

I already have my plan for the last one. As in what needs to leave my house once its done. So far, the cold cap machine needs to go the day of or after, the clothes that I wear through treatment, woolly socks, jumper, cardigan, all need to go.

Once I am out of the woods and dressed and all that, all my white cotton pj's need to go. I can't even look at these things without feeling very sick.

Not long, not long, not long, not long....

So, I started the day with the lovely Beccy, who incidentally makes the best curry's in the world, getting a second opinion on the house that I so want to buy but have the little stumbling block of selling mine first,

that or winning the lottery. She loved it as much as me. What will be will be and all that, it's in the hands of the house fairies now, lets hope they want to be kind to me.

And then a glorious day of just me. Miss Daisy was busy on her BMX, running rings around Dave last I heard, we think she's got this cycling thing down. So I had the day to myself which was just what I needed. To make some room in my head for life after chemotherapy. I'm even excited about writing that down, let alone it being just around the corner. I don't care if I have to drag myself through that last treatment, or next weeks, I will be the cold cap wearing, slightly drugged girl who has nearly finished chemo and that makes me very happy.

My head has been full of possibilities rather than questions today and dare I say the pain from within me has had a little break, I know it will probably pop back from time to time but this is the first day I can remember it not being there for absolutely months. So far, September is looking good.

So my rock and roll today has been full of me, with no pain. I like.

2nd September 2013

So far I like September. This is the first month in the last nine I have had two clear days of no pain inside me, you know that funny pain that's full of expectant panic.

It seems to have left me and in its place is a bit of a gap. I'm not sure what's going to fill this new gap of mine but let's hope its something much more desirable than its predecessor.

So today, the last day of the summer holidays, was nice and easy. Miss Daisy and me went to Attingham Park, just for a change, with the gorgeous Gaby and her friend Jane and the kids for a walk and lunch with the deer's and the rest of Shropshire it seemed.

I left them all there as Una from the Saturdays was coming to see me for my tox visit. Although I never thought I would say this about a chemotherapy nurse, I do always enjoy her visits, except those with the needles that is, as she has this peculiar calming influence on me and always talks so much sense which leaves me feeling happy and free from nonsense in my head.

All was well with my visit, still have a good head of hair, blood pressure good, no adverse side effects apart from my super sensitive veins so all looking good for next week.

Anyway, I am feeling like the end is just around the corner of this chemotherapy nonsense and dare I say I have a very little bit of excitement bubbling up inside of me. It's an apprehensive sort of excitement as let's face it, there hasn't been too much to get me going on the good side recently so I am not quite used to this feeling.

However, I shall go with this niceness and see where it takes me. Thirty-one days and counting and I move, quite swiftly, into post chemotherapy life, I can't bloody wait.

So, a BMX bike ride with Miss Daisy and gin Jayne and James to finish off my second pain free day. Perfect.

My rock and roll today has been of the good kind, full of expectant gaps and niceness.

3rd September 2013

Today is one month exactly to the end of my treatment. Hurray! Today I have had a third pain free day. Another hurray! Today I have not let those who have tried their hardest to take away my smile and, dare I say, newly found happiness succeed. When faced with adversity my pesky pain would normally make a speedy return to the place it has called home for such a long time. It seems it may have realised that the locks have now been changed.

So, September is still looking good. Even though I have spent the last hour crying over said adversity, they were tears of disbelief over inner fear or sadness. I have cried a few oceans of fearful tears this year as these last few months have been of the worst kind in almost every aspect of my life, excluding my friends, work and Miss Daisy kind of course,

but everything else has been life changingly rubbish. I can't actually find a word that portrays how bad, but I think we all get the picture. I'm nearly through the worst of it.

So said adversity above has done me a favour today, I doubt very much that was the intention.

So, Miss Daisy made it into Year One without too much drama, always good. Attingham Park made it into my daily routine which is also always good. I had a good walk with the gorgeous Gaby and her friend Jane and of course the one and only Saxon. And then I had Miss Mary with her magical hands work her massaging magic on my feet. It was heavenly. I lay there and thought non stop about what I was going to do when my chemotherapy finished. This is progress. I have not had this state of mind since December last year, you know the sort that to do with cancer or chemotherapy and nothing that requires too much decision making, like the life depending decisions I have had the joy of making this year.

That happy feeling knowing that all is going to be good, potentially anyway, is rather pleasing! I thought I had forgotten how to have these kind of crazy thoughts. Of course actions speak louder than words and as I can't yet fulfil any of my crazy dreams I shall have to trust that once I can, I will, safe in the knowledge that nothing or no one can put me back in that horrible bubble of pain. Ever.

So, my rock and roll today has been full of no nonsense determination and magically making progress.

4th September 2013

Today I was saved by an angel, of the gorgeous Gaby   variety. She well and truly saved my mood from going to a place that is not nice, not good and not

recommended. I started the day realising that I am still fragile, that   my invisible wounds have not yet healed and I need to stop getting ahead of myself. I do have a tendency to get carried away, I know, hard to believe, and so far September has given me a vision of hope that I haven't had for so   long.

Yesterday's said adversity made me doubt myself and doubt how I was doing and made me stop and think and question myself. Believe me I have done a lot of this. No one tells you when you get cancer that it also means you question everything in your whole life and everything you   once believed about yourself. Of course it makes sense that you would and as long as no big decisions are made until out of the other side all is well. Apart from the   fact it's utterly exhausting.

So, luckily, the gorgeous Gaby came to the rescue, took me for a walk around Attingham Park and helped me sort my head out. Just what I needed. We concluded that of course I am still fragile, I've not even finished

chemotherapy yet and then I get to hang out with Dan the boob man and the rest of his gang and although I am sure they are all very nice I am   a little apprehensive about having a sleepover at their hospital. I still have this blooming fuzzy brain thing going   on as well. I swear it takes me twice as long to get anything done or anything thought about which is mighty frustrating for a girl like me.

So another crisis averted, we're getting good at this. I do look forward to a time when we don't have to avert quite so many crisis in such a short period of time and I am really hoping that some good things are on my horizon that don't involve quite so much drama. A bit of drama can be quite good   fun but I really have taken this a little bit too far

now!   Anyway, I have the joy of Mr. Blinky Eyes tomorrow. However,

I am looking forward to showing him my fullish head of   hair. He

laughed when I last saw him about me having any left on this visit. In

your face Mr. Blinky Eyes! I get to report my side effects which I am very

happy to say are minimal. I did get my first mouth ulcer today but it went

as quick as it came. I upped my glass of green goodness and it seems to

have done the job. I was worrying that the   toxic nonsense was taking its

toll but it seems I have averted that crisis too.

So, my rock and roll today has been filled with the savior of my soul.

Thank the heavenly winged wonders for such friends with clever crisis

averting skills.

5th September 2013

September, so far is shaping up to be a good month. I am possibly getting

carried away with myself with it being only day five. But even with said

adversity the other day I had an angel who saved me so the crisis was

averted. I have

remained pain free, had some enlightening moments, have fallen for a fab

house and kept any unwanted side effects at bay quite successfully. The

best bit of course is the clock that is now ticking away quite nicely

meaning chemo time is nearly up.

And today, the goodness continued to flow. I had my morning walk with

the angelic gorgeous Gaby which is just the best way to start the day. I

had a bit of a revelation. I have come a longer way in my head than I thought. What I would have done or feel a matter of weeks ago I would not now. The self doubting, fearful, painful and frankly quite random nonsense that was in my head then is leaving me. I am being dumped by self doubt, ditched by fearful pain and quite random nonsense has run for the hills. A break up I am happy about and I hope I can politely tell them where to go if they ever come back.

So, with a spring in my step and feeling a little lighter now the freeloaders have done one, I head off to see Mr. Blinky Eyes. As a slight distraction,

I get to the hospital and it seemed there was a 70's convention in the waiting room. I have never seen so many old people dressed randomly in shiny white shoes, white flares, blue jackets and hair pieces. And that was just the men.

Anyway, Mr. Binky Eyes was his usual happy, chatty self. Not. I opened by asking him what he though of my hair. He really does not know how to take me. He laughed uncomfortably and scribbled it down whilst saying it out loud 'still has hair'. But, the very good news was that I am doing very well. He even suggested I do not see him again I am doing that well. I think at that point I may have offended him as I smiled, my biggest smile at the prospect of not seeing my oncologist again. He took it back. I have to see him one more time in October. But that is it. How exciting is that.

So, today I have been the most excited I have been since December 2012. In twenty eight days I have my last ever chemotherapy treatment. About four or five weeks after that I have my surgery. I can see an end to it. Finally. It seems chemotherapy not only renews my cells to make me well, it also renews my thought processes, priorities and gives me clarity through the fog of the choices I know I can now make in the future. The best bit is I have a future. When this started in January and again in

May there were times I thought I may not be able to say that. So now I have one I have to make sure it's a good one. A very good one. The best kind of one. One that doesn't involve things I think I should want to do but don't want to. Like gardening. I hate it. I tried. I won't again.

So, my rock and roll today has been full of getting the thumbs up from Mr. Blinky Eyes and letting my emotional freeloaders ditch me and run for the hills.

6th September 2013

So, Mr. Blinky Eyes made me   happy yesterday. He doesn't smile very much and he laughs in a very uncomfortable way. I can also imagine he's not used to someone quite as cheery as me in his office repeatedly going on about hair and still having a head full of it. I feel like I have defied the rules of chemotherapy by keeping it, of course the cold cap has done the work, I've just endured the frost bite. I sure hope it wants to go the distance with me now the end is so clearly in site.

So, on my morning walk with the angelic gorgeous Gaby we again put the world to rights, or I should say, my world to rights really. Gaby has missed her vocation in life as she could have been charging by the hour with her truly amazing words and made an absolute fortune by now.

It is a fact that I hit rock bottom and was a broken woman in every sense of the word. I guess I didn't realise how bad things were until I hit my wall with an almighty bang. I believe that's the cancer effect. The cancer effect also means you have to stop, put your life on hold and spend some time with yourself in a fuzzy headed, toxic sort of way, facing the fear amongst other things. I found that very tricky.

I was not good at hanging out with myself, something about not thinking I was overly good company. Ever the doubter. But, thanks to those who kept me smiling, Ms. Angelic's amazing words and my own ability to face the pain I have been brought back to life. So it   seems It's not just the chemotherapy that has saved me,   it appears I have done some of the saving too.

Anyway, its very tiring saving yourself along with all the toxic stuff. What a year. I am very much looking forward to waving good bye to the nonsense.

So my rock and roll has been full of heavenly winged gorgeousness and bringing me back to life.

7th September 2013

Today was a great day. It went a little like this. Miss Daisy, Dave, Gorgeous Gaby, Bella, Saxon, the fab Beccy, Amy, Alfie, Leo, Mate and Kel (Kate and Mel) Murphy, roller coasters of the carnival kind, Attingham Park,

of course, next door neighbours house and then bed.

I haven't had a day for months that has been this good fun filled with such good people. I am one lucky lady.

This day's rock and roll was filled with actual rock and roll and roller coasters. Perfect!

8th September 2013

You stole the sun from my heart, as the Manic Street Preachers sang, describes me over the last few months perfectly. Of course it's the big C that has done the stealing. I heard it on the radio today and it made me stop and think, just for a change, about how that sums me up.

I lost my sunshine.

The good news is that it's coming back, brighter than it once was. The gorgeous Gaby compared me to a butterfly the other day (and Kylie, clearly not in looks, more in reinvention) You know that I'm getting ready to spread my wings, time for the real me to come back to life, not the frightened, full of nonsense girl that I have been. So whilst I was stopping and thinking I realised it's happening. In three and a half weeks I will be having my last treatment, in ten days I see my surgeons to arrange the next and last step in all of this horribleness and I will start to get my life back, in as much as the fuzzy horribleness of chemo stops, the surgery, I know is still to come.

So, I am coming back to life, slowly but surely and it feels truly wonderful! I am so very excited that soon it all changes, for the better this time. This is a good feeling. At some points I thought the chemotherapy bit wasn't going to end, but now it feels like its just around the corner. I am a   little apprehensive, as always, about this week's treatment day, but

who wouldn't when it comes to toxic nonsense and cold cap torture.

Two left. That's all that matters.

I have amazed myself in so many ways so far through this, in the good, the very good and the not so good. When I look back I don't really know how I got myself through to this point, but I have. And I am sure I can get through the next bit that's on its way. Maybe watching a lot of really bad films has helped. One thing cancer hasn't changed is my taste in films. Spider Man, The Avengers and Columbo all featured last week. Although Stardust is on now and that is my favourite, it reminds me of Miss Daisy, I watched it when she only a few days old. She slept on me through the whole film, lovely.

So, it is soon time to stop analysing every inch of my life and start living it, this is the very best bit. I have made a promise to myself to treat myself well. And by treat, I don't mean the tasty variety, although everyone needs a good treat every now and again, I mean to look after myself well, with honesty and respect and with plenty of rock and roll. I like!

So, my rock and roll today has been full of my very own sunshine, filling that gap in my heart quite nicely.

9th September 2013

So, happily reunited with my sunshine the week begins with

my penultimate treatment at the forefront of my mind. It's a little frantic in my head. I worry that my blood tests won't come back ok, but they always have so why should this week be any different. Logic prevails a little but pesky worry can sometimes take over; I don't think there is anything wrong with that right now. I want my house to be miraculously spotless and tidy. Miss Daisy and me live in it though so there is little chance of that. The big clean starts today and by Wednesday its done. There is nothing worse that being ill, unable to move much and noticing things that need to be done, that's just annoying.

So my day starts with the gorgeous Gaby, my favourite   way. We swap our walk for a coffee and a stroll around town and we both get a little excited that in three weeks' time I will be getting ready for my last, ever, treatment. I really like saying that. I then head off for lunch with Stuart and I think we decide that even in the face of adversity it's possible to come out smiling without resorting to your default position, possibly Buddhism is the way forward and what will be will be. Simple as that. Perfect!

This week is a little like a military operation. I have no idea what part of what I am doing is working but I know something is so I dare not give any of it up just in case. Most

days I consume a fair amount of super goodness but this week is especially important to make sure I am fighting fit for the toxic nonsense. I have all my supplements, two pints of vegetable juice with of course fennel, I will be giving that a miss for a while when this is done, I have had a fennel nearly every day for the last 15 weeks. And then the green goodness that is spirulina and wheatgrass with manuka honey. This is disgusting. It works. It all takes blooming ages.

I am so looking forward to getting back to a normal. My new normal that is. It will be a relief to stop worrying about constant recovery. It will be nice to stop feeling like my hair is falling out every day, it's not really now, but until I am out of the treatment cycle anything could happen, what a bummer that would be now after all this time, fingers crossed it will go the distance. It will be nice for these very interesting hot flushes to stop, I'm far too young for those! I kept hold of my periodicals for as long as I could, I do believe they have left me now. They may make a return, who knows but these hot flushes really need to stop. Una from the Saturdays assures me they will.

So there we have it, I am longing for something that is only just around the corner. Hallelujah!

My rock and roll has been full of good people, super green goodness and getting excited. Good things come to those who wait apparently.

10th September 2013

Miss Daisy thinks I'm a dare devil. I laughed out loud. She gets this from Saturday night at the carnival when I was trying desperately to persuade my mate Leo to come on every single ride with me. Leo is 10 and rightfully declined. I have never liked roller coasters, until now it seems. Maybe it's the wanting to feel alive thing or maybe I really just haven't been out and done very much for such a long time that a roller coaster seems a good option. I sure hope I come to my senses and don't start hanging out at Alton Towers at every given opportunity.

So, whilst having a bath this morning, Miss Daisy sat and talked to me, as usual, this time about being a dare devil and she declared with some passion that when my boobies are no longer blue, unbelievably they still are, and my treatment is over, not long now, then we can be dare devils together. This could be dangerous, but very much fun all at the same time. I think I like the sound of this.

Anyway, my day started with the amazing Amanda and her magic massaging hands. Part of it was a birthday treat and the rest was my usual reflexology goodness. It was

glorious. I woke myself up with what can only be described as a snort. Oh dear! I had fallen asleep and had some crazy dreams in the short time my eyes were closed. Clearly her hands really are magic as that's a first for me. Awake or not it was glorious all the same.

Then off to Attingham Park with the gorgeous Gaby for our daily walk. Another glorious part of my day. However, tired I feel this walk just does the job, partly the exercise and partly the wonderfulness of the gorgeous Gaby and Saxon, good for my soul.

So, Georgie Fame is heading my way tomorrow to take my blood to make sure I am ready for Thursday. At this point I always worry that it might not be. I can't see why it won't be but you just never know. Georgie Fame was the nurse that saved my hair with the suggestion of a mild sedative throughout my treatment, which I have ready and waiting, and when she called me she remembered it was my nearly last treatment and even she sounded a little excited for me!

I am very excited; I will be even more so when I get the go ahead for this week. I do like to stay on track, especially for something like this, it consumes every inch of my waking mind.

So, whilst Miss Daisy was having her bath this evening, I was sat talking to her, clearly a family tradition, and she started to talk about my hair, my treatment and going for walks.

I said I can't walk for a few days after my treatment so I make the most of it before. And then out of nowhere she cried, a lot. It was the thought of me not being well and the   tough understanding of why that got to her. It was probably in her head from the blue boobies this morning.

She cried. And cried. I reminded her of being a dare devil and she smiled. Crisis averted. At least it's coming out. I haven't got it straight in my head yet how on earth I explain to her   about mastectomies and reconstruction, she knows more ouchy boobies are on the way, that will do for now.

So my very excitable rock and roll today has been full   of magic massaging hands, the saving of my soul whilst walking and Miss Daisy getting it all out and being a dare devil for all the right reasons.

Penultimate treatment, here I come. I am good to go   for tomorrows toxic nonsense. It's a very mixed bag of feelings about this today. I woke up wanting to cry, in fact I had all on holding it together at the school drop off and rushed out of there with my head down as soon as Miss Daisy would let go of my leg and trot off for her day of learning. I wanted to go in with her and sit in the class and pretend I was 5 again. That may have been a little odd, so I took myself off to try very hard to talk my self around and out of the place I was heading.

It turned out that I had no time to wallow, big relief, as Georgie Fame arrived bang on time and my boss James emailed me averting my attention from the dark place to a much better place which was good. I do like seeing Ms. Fame, she's full of the caring, calming, specialness that all the nurses I have come across with my chemo have been. She also remembered lots about me and Miss Daisy and has had the amazingness to start reading all the nonsense that I write down on a daily basis to get myself through all of this.

So, still impressed with my hair and my positiveness and the fact that after tomorrow I only have three weeks left of chemo, hurray! we crack on with the blood taking and run through any lasting side effects (I have none apart from the lack of brain thing) and then we chat. I love to chat with Ms. fame, I never thought I would say that about a nurse taking my blood ready for me to have chemotherapy.

As Georgie Fame heads off to America, nice, I head off to the doctors. I'm seeing a doctor I haven't seen in years, the first thing he says to me is he is not used to my change of name. How random! But as Gaby did point out at least he knew me, not like Mr. Blinky Eyes who had to call my name in an empty waiting room with only me there. Anyway, he started to ask me about being tested for the BRACA 1 gene and then

getting Daisy tested. This is the test to see if I have the breast cancer gene. I wasn't ready for this conversation today; I had gone for something completely different. I can't bare the thought of Miss Daisy having to go through anything as horrible as this. I hope I am doing it for both of us and it never touches her. Of course by the time she needs to worry research may have discovered all sorts of things, christ, there may even be something crazy like a cure for cancer, or is that me just being plain silly. I will of course get tested, just not today.

So, then off for our daily walk to Attingham Park with the gorgeous Gaby and Saxon, always perfect. I am being a tad random as I always am the day before the toxic stuff. I get Gaby to check my head for bald patches in the cafe, a busy cafe, must have looked quite bizarre.

There were none. I start to fret about my blood not being ready and what will I do if it doesn't happen tomorrow. Gaby calmed me. I go to get Miss Daisy and at home I am organising and tidying in a frantic sort of way.

Miss Daisy, clearly bored of me, bakes a cake around me, how did I not notice what she was doing. I managed to turn things on like ovens and mixers without really being aware, before I knew it there was a chocolate cake waiting for me. Clever Miss Daisy! That was tasty.

My evening of franticness continues and no doubt will do well into the night. I have been saved a little by Ben gossiping with me over WhatsApp, just like this morning I was saved a little by my boss James emailing me shocked I was getting a little restless and of course Ms. Fame's lovely chats and the gorgeous Gaby's calmness. Little things can change the direction of my mood so easily on days like today.

Una from the Saturdays will be winging her way to me with her needles in the morning along with the gorgeous Gaby to get me through the day

So, my rock and roll today has been full of nervous randomness, being saved by people who had no idea they were saving me and being good to go for the penultimate one. See you on the other side ready for my 21-day countdown.

13th September 2013

Treatment number five is over and out. Phew! Let the countdown to the end of chemotherapy begin.

Twenty days and counting and I am most definitely over and out of what is the most unbelievably hard and challenging thing I have ever had to do and I hope I ever have to do. I know it is making me a whole person physically and emotionally and I hope and pray it means cancer will never

darken my door again, but boy it's a toughie. The good news is, of course, I only have one more left. So, my day yesterday started in a frantic way. I was up at five only because I couldn't sleep and I re cleaned all the floors and rugs and anything I could think off all before Miss Daisy woke up.

She then demanded we both watch Scooby doo in bed which, of course, we did and it did the treat calming me down. Then time for Miss Daisy to go and not be back with me for four days which is far too long but very necessary as she would not be happy with me like this and would ultimately be bored. And who could blame her, there is only so much being in bed and watching rubbish TV anyone can do. Magnum PI, The Professionals, NCIS LA and of course Hawaii 5 0 all have been on today whilst I have been in and out of sleep.

Anyway, I take my happy pills to calm me right down and get me in the chemotherapy zone, gorgeous Gaby arrives and we try and get our heads into what's coming.

I think I am a bit more emotional on this one and feel like it may not go quite as well as the last one, but as I have no choice in the matter it was time to power on through.

Una from the Saturdays arrives and with her is another chemo nurse to observe. Bit of a curve ball but luckily Selina,

now affectionately named Celine Dion, was lovely and basically got her boobs out. More on that later!

Treatment starts, cold cap on, post man comes and I get a little bag of happiness from the lovely and very thoughtful Sarah which was absolutely perfect timing and possibly got me through the rest of the treatment with   a smile on face. Along with everything Gaby was doing and the lovely chat from the nurses. Apart from a few tears that is, out if nowhere and feeling very sick until the cap came off, but that soon passed when my body got back to temperature, how random. I felt sick all the way through this time, but I think I do on every one. Only one more time.

So, Celine Dion it turns out shared her very personal story with Gaby and I and Una from The Saturdays about having a double mastectomy and reconstruction four and a half months ago. Me and Gaby had only just been talking about it in the morning as we need to write down questions for the surgeon as there are so many.

It seems we could ask all we wanted to Celine Dion and she was very happy to chat and get them out! Just as she left she gave us all a look and we were all so impressed and It felt a whole lot better about the next phase of this nonsense. Clearly she was meant to come to my house that day.

So, today I'm in bed, feeling sick. I get my very necessary lovely visit from the lovely Christine which is a great part of

this day as I get out of bed for a couple of hours and   chat. I actually never remember what about and I am sure I make no sense, but bless her she doesn't mind! I get messages from lovely people which keeps me going on days like this. Robin from the MAB massive decided I reminded him of Samantha Womack. I have been compared to   a number of things recently, gorgeous Gaby told me I was a weeble that wobbled but did fall down! I preferred the butterfly and Kylie ones. I'm happy with Samantha Womack too as it goes, soon (ish) my hair will be that long again. I can live in hope anyway. Clearly I look nothing like them, but all the same its nice.

So, a night of staying in bed awaits, my plan is to sleep my way through this day. Nessa (BF) is winging her way to   me tomorrow which is just great.

So my rock and roll is again people saving me without even knowing it, the gorgeous Gaby getting me through that day, Miss Daisy being a swot like her mum and only having twenty days left of this nonsense.

Time for this girl to sleep.

14th September 2013

Nineteen days and I will be finished on this wonderfully   terrible chemotherapy journey. As I sit here with the lovely Nessa (BF) getting waves of excitement, along

with waves of blooming hot flushes, from my sofa about being able to see the end of this bit, by far the worse bit of the treatment, it does start to feel I have the beginnings of coming back to life.

It is fair to say that I have been holding myself together, or not at times, to get through these last sxsteen weeks which of course feels like about 160 years to me, but now I can feel myself unravelling. In a good way. The hot flushes are a side effect by the way, a false state of menopause which I am   not particularly enjoying. Funny that.

Una from the Saturdays assures me they will stop after the treatment; I hope she is right.

So, yesterday I did as planned and slept through most of it, apart from the odd Magnum PI and Hawaii 5 0 of   course. Very annoyingly I woke up at 2.30am and couldn't go back to sleep, so had various scenarios running through my head of what I shall be getting up to in a few weeks' time and I probably got myself into such a happy state of mind that I really couldn't sleep.

I did eventually and managed to stay in bed until after lunch today. Perfect.

Ready for Nessa to keep me company on my sofa watching crap TV and deciding on what we shall all be getting up to

very very very soon.   So, I still can't move very much and I still feel a little odd but I do think I am slightly better this afternoon than I have been in previous treatments. I think the key is not moving and Nessa being here! Just what I needed. Oh and we just discovered magnum minis in the freezer!

So, my rock and roll today is full of Nessa (BF), not moving much and realising very slowly that I may just be coming back to life. The butterfly effect remember.

Alex Jagger

<u>15th September 2013</u>

18 weeks ago, today as it goes, I had just found my second lot of cancer, Nessa was with me on that fateful day and it was mighty surreal and very scary. However, in 18 days' time I will be having my last ever chemotherapy treatment, and Nessa is with me again today. A much better day! I am coming out of this last treatment quite nicely, still physically the same as I guess that doesn't change as it's the same amount of toxic nonsense every time, but much better emotionally. A little clearer in my head. More on that later.

So, I decided this morning whilst lying in bed that I have a bit in common with Britney Spears. She after all sang about being toxic. I am toxic. For very different reasons as I am sure she wasn't singing about chemotherapy. She then lost her mind and cut off all her hair. I also lost my mind and cut off all my hair, albeit under much

more dignified circumstances, the hair cutting that is, the losing of my mind was most undignified. My hair cutting involved champagne, tears and friends, I believe hers involved clippers with mad eyes. Anyway, that is clearly where the similarity ends. Just one of my early morning observations, I have many.

Anyway, on being clearer in my head. Something has happened today that hasn't happened since the chemotherapy started. I seem to have some of brain   back. Hallelujah! I have been thinking and scheming and trying very hard to find ways to secure the future I so crave for me and

Daisy for when this is over. It has sure helped that Nessa has decided to stay another day, hurray! She has patiently listened to me rattle off numbers and sums and conniving ways of getting to where I want to be. Of course a fillet steak and a chicken roast dinner helped. But all the same this has been exciting as I haven't just got frustrated at the lack of brain power and given up which is usual story, and I have actually started something and think I have come to a conclusion.

Lets not get carried away. I have, though, really enjoyed this new brain power feeling and loved Nessa staying another day to help me get to grips with using this new brain power thing. It so seems like this is all getting a little   real. You know, the

lovely end to chemo, something that seemed such a long way off now seems just around the corner. We have both had wonderful waves of excitement about that today. I like. A lot.

So my very lovely rock and roll today has been filled with the joys of Nessa, fillet steak and having a brain. Perfect.

16th September 2013

So, my countdown continues to the last ever treatment and my brain is coming back to life, slowly but surely. I have to say I like this feeling very much. Even though thinking about having my treatment makes me feel super sick and makes my veins twinge, I will drag myself kicking and screaming to that day if I have to, as the prize on the other side has been keeping me going. You know the prize I have had my eye on for the last

16 weeks. The finishing line. Or the start to getting myself back to being me again.

So, when I think back to a time when I wrote this   blog when not under the influence of toxic nonsense, it was when I was just about holding myself

 together by a fine thread of nothingness. It was those fateful two weeks before this treatment started that I decided to write to help me get through. I look back now and I feel like a completely different person. A person who has nearly

conquered the art of getting through chemotherapy. I'm not quite there yet but what's seventeen days in the grand scale of things.

Nothing compared to the last sixteen weeks I can tell you. This is quite an unusual feeling, not one I have experienced before and I am not entirely sure where it's going to take me, but it feels unbelievably lovely to know that I am soon out of this bit. It feels super exciting.

Anyway, today started with me trying to buy a house. As you do. I've not got there quite yet but where there is a will there is a way I do believe. Of course it would help if my house fairies got it together and sold the one I have first. You never know, they may be just about to jump into action as we speak. What will be will be and all that but there's no harm in a little intervention at times.

So, Nessa headed back to Leeds and I headed back into daily walking with the gorgeous Gaby and Saxon, not bad four days after the toxic stuff.

We had to stop first so we could eat, or so I could eat before we walked. I had forgotten how much I actually eat at this time, it is ridiculous, but clearly very necessary. Food, in fact, took over the day.

Miss Daisy came home and we cooked, we ate, I ate more. You get the picture.

So, I have a big spring in my step about having my surgical appointment on Wednesday. I never thought I would be quite so happy to see my surgeon, the one who normally tells me I have cancer, but not this time. This time he   will hopefully be telling me when my surgery will be or something along those lines. The last chapter in this not so pleasant book I am currently playing the staring role. But of course this is the best chapter. It's the one that ends with me being heathy and whole again, in every sense of the word, so all good. I may even get to meet up with James (MAB massive) on the same day, so even better.

So, my very excitable rock and roll today has been full of the two lovelies Nessa and Gaby, wheeling and dealing on   the housing front and basking in the warm glow of seventeen days and it's done.

<u>17th September 2013</u>

There are very few people who can wake me up at 5.30am to try and make me laugh and get away with it. Miss Daisy is of course one of them. She woke me up telling me she wanted to wear her mittens. This was to make me laugh. It worked (you had to be there). Who knows what happens in that little girl's mind! So that was us up. We watched Scooby doo in bed until it was time for school. Not a bad start to the day.

Another good start to the day was home made biscuits from

the lovely Helen. Unbelievably tasty. Nothing better than being thought about.

The daily walk was rained off today so it morphed into a meeting of a mutual bedding fetish for me and Gaby and coffee. Perfect. I think we both had moments throughout the day of realising that this treatment stuff will be over really soon. We both agreed it will be very surreal. Not like the usual anti climax feeling that sometimes happens, or the holiday blues, or anything I know actually. More like this is the start of something wonderful.

The other funny thing that happened today was   me realising that I have had cancer. I know this sounds really stupid, after all that's all I have gone on about all year. It is getting very boring. I know. But, as I lay in bed this morning, remembering the most random of dreams about having curly ginger hair, one dream I don't really want to come true, it hit me that I have actually nearly done this thing. The cancer thing. That is having it, getting through the treatment, getting over it and moving on. That thing. I felt a little smug.

So, after buying duvet covers and drinking coffee I wound my way to Mary with her magical massaging hands to look after my feet. It was heavenly as always. All I could think about throughout the magical massaging though was steak. Eating steak that is. Crazy girl that I am.

So, I bought steak on the way home and for the first time ever, in the history of Alex Jagger, I cooked myself steak with all manor of other tasty treats. I even used my dads steak knives that I doubt have been out of the box for over 25 years. I smiled all the way through eating it and wondered why it's taken me so long to do such a lovely thing. Maybe because I am not this obsessed with eating such food in normal times. As I have no idea what normal means anymore, maybe these steak knives will see the light of day a little more in the future.

Anyway, my Mr. Cautious surgeon awaits tomorrow morning, I so hope I get a date, of the surgical kind that is. I know I need to be prepared for not getting one, but all the same,   it would be nice. I have the gorgeous Gaby with me to remember to ask any boob related questions that I may forget. These meetings can be a little tricky at times and I can get stuck on words or emotions and then miss the rest, not good. Fingers crossed.

So, my rock and roll today has been full of smug steak, one of the best girls, biscuits and magical massaged feet all wrapped up in blissful blankets.

ps. Christmas is everywhere. This is possibly the only year I will be happy about it being this early, but boy, it is making me one happy girl.

18th September 2013

Today has been a good day for two reasons. I got a date and Miss Daisy lost her first tooth.

So, firstly my date. 6th November. Surgery booked. I am very happy. I had all sorts of worries this morning (not like me) that I would walk away from the meeting none the   wiser and just fall back into a world of fluffy uncertainty. But no. Me and the gorgeous Gaby were taken a back at the swiftness and organisation of what's coming next. What a relief. Miss Silver pixie boots was there, aka Wendy my breast care nurse, and of course my surgeon who I managed to launch myself at again, I don't think he minds anymore. Everyone was impressed at my head of hair and that so far I am doing well. I did have to ask Miss Pixie to stop telling me how well I had done as I thought I was going to cry, but worse, I thought she was going to cry.

So, I am seeing Dan the boob man on Friday to go into the detail and agree the type of reconstruction I will be having. I am not having both mastectomies done at the same time as my skin is too thin on the first side due to radiotherapy, this one will be done next year. This is fine as really it's down to risk. Weighing up the risks the first time around was the straw that broke my back and put me firmly on the path to my very undignified loss of mind, but this time is different.

Having chemotherapy has just given me an extra 10% on the risk front. I did have an 80% chance of cancer not recurring, this has now increased to 90%. The pain has been worth it. The risk on the first side is already lower,   after surgery in November the risk will be the same for both sides. I am having the mastectomy next year because it takes the fear away. As long as I have breast tissue I have fear. I have been given a booklet to read before Friday that goes through what my options are.

This has slightly freaked me out I have to say. I decided to stop reading it and wait for Dan the boob expert to advise me. One thing I do know is, it will all be good. The results are amazing and I will have the fear taken away. So, it's going to take a little longer for   all surgeries, but that I can get on with life rather than being in the horrible suspended state of chemotherapy.

So, I came away from the hospital feeling relieved. In fact, gorgeous Gaby said she could see the change in my face as the morning progressed. It feels odd, in a good way, that I can finally see what is happening. I have surgery, stay in hospital for a few days, have a few weeks' recovery and then go back to work. By the time the one next year comes around I will be so well rehearsed in this that it will be a walk in the park. Easy. All day today I have felt very oddly excited. I'm looking forward to seeing James next week to talk about coming back to work and how it will happen and when. This is good news.

Anyway, enough of me, the other big news was the tooth that finally escaped from the jaws of Miss Daisy. A very momentous moment and a very happy little girl. The tooth fairy needs to make sure she can find her way to her bed tonight or there will be trouble. So all in all a very big day for the girls today.

So, my rock and roll today has been full of dates for new boobs, getting giddy with the gorgeous Gaby and Miss Daisy staying awake to see the tooth fairy.

19th September 2013

There are many phrases that I use to describe days like   today. Such as
'sick of the whole damn shooting match' or 'it's all relative to the Tibetan
monks'. One thing I have learnt through all of this, is that moods, mainly
mine, can change at the flick of a light switch, so clearly I'm still more
fragile than I had given myself credit for. It may have been the 5.30am
news this morning stating that cancer is incurable that started me off, or it
could have been my ability to give myself a really hard time for things
that I should be letting myself off the hook for by now, that plague me on
days like today, or the fact I have the headache from hell, have no taste
buds, am a strange sort of tired, am not enjoying constant hot flushes at
all, have veins that resemble bones not veins, have realised brain coming
back takes time and generally have forgotten, today, what the hell I am
doing.

So, life usually happens around you whilst you're busy getting on with it,
unless of course your name is Alex Jagger. For me, life is right in my face,
every single thing I've ever done wrong or not been happy with comes
back to haunt me on days like today. Of course this does happen to
everyone, we all have bad days and bad times and it's all relative to what's
happening in life, at that time, for that person. I was on a roll, September
so far has been good and today I have taken myself by surprise that I feel
quite so wobbly. Maybe its because I can see the clock moving moving
now and I can see some much needed light. This is making me happy, I
promise, but I also want it to be now. Ms. Impatient here can almost

touch a life out of this horrible suspended state and I would be very happy if I was getting up in the morning and going to work and doing all manor of day to day stuff. Maybe its because my brain is coming back and I want it to be back to full working order now. It isn't and it takes time, apparently.

All I have done this year is wait for my body or brain or emotional state to improve, recover or regenerate.

Anyway, I took myself off for a walk to the usual haunt to try and clear my head. I may have been talking to myself in the woods, trying to have a word with myself and get myself away from the dark place

I was heading to fast. I did vow to stop giving myself a hard time for being a bit of a twat at times earlier this year. I had cancer. I didn't know how to handle it. That should be enough to excuse myself from adverse behaviour and stop beating myself up so many months on. No one else is worrying about any stupidity back then so god only knows why I still am. I also vowed to just get my head down now and get through this next few weeks.

My life will not return to its new normal until I am back doing my normal stuff. If I can even remember what my normal stuff is. But I do know it is not normal to be having chemotherapy, recover from chemotherapy and then to float through the days running up to the next chemotherapy in a bit of a self analytical haze. It is not normal to be getting ready for major surgery. It is also not normal to be seeing a psychologist to make sure I can cope with the surgery. This is just a formality due to the type of surgery and reconstruction, but all the same, this psychologist may well have a field day with me!

Maybe people say that the last treatment is the worst due to this kind of mind fuck, nothing to do with how harsh it is physically. You know the lure of what you can nearly have, but not quite yet. I just want mine and Miss Daisy's normal back. Please.

So, whilst walking and beating myself up with that really big stick I insist on having by my side, I was saved. Again by someone who had no idea they were saving me. Just a simple message took me out of myself and made me see that I   was actually doing alright. It is a funny thing and a moving thing. I don't feel the same as I did a matter of weeks ago although I am very possibly saying very similar things, as this is all new. This is seeing myself in the future and wanting to be there now.

Clearly I have not learnt to be that   patient. We don't know what it is going to feel like to go through this sort of nonsense, unless we do. I had no idea before, even though I had lost people to this. I had no idea how I would deal with it, day to day and all the rest of it. Single girl with a five-year-old daughter lost in a world of dealing with it physically and emotionally and trying desperately to keep things as normal as possible for the light of my life.

That I have done. Miss Daisy is doing good, apart from being bored of it now. This is thanks to all of us, me, Dave and all these good people around me. We may be a dysfunctional family but it's one that sure works. I am lucky. Very lucky. I have all these good people around me, near or far, close or distant, who save me on a regular basis without even knowing it.

The rest of it, well, faced with being sliced and diced is not a tricky part, although it is a big part. It feels like a formality and a stay in hospital, I just want my life back now please. I want to be me, for being me, not for having cancer or fear free   boobs. Not too much to ask, surely.

So, its fair to say, today I am sick of the whole damn shooting match. Oh and I get to be naked from the waste up for a whole new person tomorrow, just in the name of medicine.

My rock and roll today is full of not so rock and roll, being saved to remember I am doing alright, even on a bad day and being blessed with the light of my life.

ps. Miss Daisy and me baked and baked and baked some more. It worked.

20th September 2013

So, today being a new day, I do the decent thing and indulge in some retail therapy. For new boobs. It was of course my day with Dan the Boob Man. But, for the first time since this treatment has started I felt really ill. Clearly I feel really ill straight after my treatment but so far I have stayed well outside of those times. This morning I woke up with the headache from hell again and felt very sick. I just   about managed to get Miss Daisy to school, but that was touch and go, and I got myself home and back to bed. This is sort of what I have been dreading and so far escaped.

Mr. Blinky Eyes did tell me I would feel   more fatigue towards the end of the treatment. I do - that's for sure, but I have not felt like I did this morning. Sleep fixed it enough for me to drive to sort out my impending surgery.

So, Dan the Boob man was very good and made me feel a whole lot better about what is going to happen. I had diagrams, pictures, he sat staring at me for ages naked from the waste up doing measurements and describing exactly what will happen and what the end results will be. And the end results will be good, I now feel confidant about that. I was with him well over an hour which took me by surprise. The meetings I have had to date have been quick and to   the point, I think anyway. So I left feeling good about what will happen. It's all booked in and sorted and it feels very real. It feels like really soon I shall be back doing what I do, whatever that may be. I really can't remember its been so blooming long!

I headed off to see the gorgeous Gaby to talk boobs. On the way there I realised my headache had gone and I started to feel better. I wonder if I was a little stressed. Anyway, Gaby was suitably impressed with my boob plan, we had a quick coffee, a quick chat and I had a quick squeeze with the very lovely Saxon and off we both went. I felt better.

Whilst on my way home for Miss Daisy I had a little   think. Again, not like me. I decided to take matters into my own hands and try and just get on with what I want to do for me, Miss Daisy and those in my life to make sure we all have a good time, have fun, laugh a lot and not get bogged down with all the crap, whilst getting on with life in general. I'm sure this sounds very idealistic, it is, but I don't care, it is possible and I will make it happen. I am getting rid of my big stick that I have had by my side for so long, its very last of season and now goes with nothing I have. I'm going to burn it, along with all the other cancer related stuff when this is done.

Anyway, I'm bored of feeling like I am bogged down by all this crap. Of course I am, I have had no choice, but enough already. Bring on Dan the boob man and his merry band of surgeons. When they arrive it means it's nearly over and normal life can resume.

I'm off to bed, I'm feeling the fatigue.

So my rock and roll today has been full of boobs, quick chats to bring me back to life and taking matters into my own hands.

22nd September 2013

So, safe in the knowledge that my boobs are going to be in safe hands, so to speak,

I have relaxed more this weekend. I have relaxed more because it's all arranged and sorted out and I am not anxiously waiting for something to happen. I am also relaxing because my countdown is going well. I have had a few bad days recently, it has to be said, but I have had far more good ones. By the time my chemotherapy finishes and I have recovered, had my surgery and recovered and got back to work, it will have been one whole year that I have been dealing with having cancer. Not surprised I am now very bored of it.

My very unlucky 2013, that started on December 9th 2012. The day I found my first lump. I will never, ever forget it. Who knew that all this was to follow. I certainly have been to hell and back a few times, that's for sure. But as Fleetwood Mac would say, don't stop thinking about tomorrow, no point in looking back. And how do I know this. Miss Daisy has decided that it's her new favourite song. She sings it to me.

So, my weekend has been full of sunshine, gorgeous Gaby, lots of kids, parks, Scooby doo, next door neighbours sleeping in the flower beds and back to back films whilst feeling the fatigue. I have been so tired today that as soon as Miss Daisy was off, I parked myself on the sofa and watched films, I cried at all of them.

Anyway, eleven days to go. I can't quite believe it. I have something to do on every one of these days and, as I am tireder than a very tired thing, bed is never far away. Eleven days and I can put the chemotherapy behind me, get rid of all the chemotherapy associated stuff and let the fog lift. I cannot blooming well wait.

So my very tired rock and roll today has been full of films, crying at all of them and feeling good about only having eleven days left of the toxic stuff.

23rd September 2013

It appears I have staged my very own revolution, against myself and what this thing does to me at times. The last week has been tough. Strange really as I am so close to the end of this unbelievably testing time, that surely I should be shouting from the roof tops and jumping for joy at any given opportunity. But no, I am not. I had fallen off my very healthy wagon temporarily. I am rather disappointed with myself as yesterday I could feel mouth ulcers starting, heartburn starting and generally I felt exhausted.

Luckily I had only fallen off it for 3 days and I have now jumped right back on and this morning all those pesky side effects have gone. Classic side effects are heartburn, mouth ulcers and of course hair loss. I have, to some degree, escaped all of these, I'm not about to let my own stubbornness change that now.

So today its time to get back on it and power on through. It seems the last few days can be quite tricky. Maybe because it's so close but yet so far that's really frustrating, or   because nearly one year of doing what I am doing is really too much, maybe I wanted to pretend I was normal, well let's face it I'm never going to be normal, but normal in terms of living without having cancer or maybe I was just too tired to be super woman. Really, I just need to get over myself. I now have.

So, today I am going to make the house look like it's not been burgled, yes I have neglected everything, go for a walk, get back on the healthy trail, paint my nails, it always helps, I have no idea why and get ready to see Una from the Saturdays for my tox visit. She will put me back on the right path too, she always does. Next week I am having my last treatment, bloody hallelujah! Start with the end in mind and all that, I am nearly there, that's what I need to keep in mind. Ten sleeps and counting.

So, I am planning a bit more rock and roll today of the 'getting back on it' variety and being the master of picking myself up of the floor.

24th September 2013

Nine sleeps. That's my news today, I am in single figures. From 126 to 9 days left of chemotherapy, woo hoo!

So, my day yesterday and today has been filled with the gorgeous Gaby, my Nessa (BF), Mary's magical massaging hands, the lovely Beccy, Una from The Saturdays with Celine Dion, Miss Daisy and 3-mile power walks around Attingham Park, after 18 weeks of chemo, am I mad!

Coffee, chatting, houses, and my toxicity visit from Una from the Saturdays. All is well with my recovery, in fact all is very good so far, Una is happy with me and she put me straight on the whole getting to the end of this nonsense, helping me get over myself.

It's normal apparently.

Power walking, magical massaged feet, I woke myself up not once, but twice snoring. Was that me, I thought, surely not. It was. Not a good look. Magical Mary found it hilarious. Booking hair appointments for 4 weeks time, lovely lunch with Nessa (BF) and generally hanging out with one of my best girls, the perfect way to spend the day.   Tomorrow I'm back to power walking, even though every muscle in my body is saying don't do it. I'm walking my way to day zero.

My rock and roll today have been full of the best people and being in single figures. Hallelujah!

25th September 2013

Now, I'm not sure I've mentioned that it's my last treatment

next week. Eight sleeps and I'm done. That's next week, a   week

tomorrow to be exact.

Today, it seems I have been dropping this into conversation as much as I

possibly can. Anyone would think I am a bit pleased with myself. I am in

fact very pleased with myself, along with being full of relief, disbelief with

a sort of surreal anticipation that feels like it could be the start of

something wonderful.

This is also my 100th blog, how time doesn't fly   when you're not having

fun. It feels like so much longer to me. That's ok as one week tomorrow I

shall be welcoming Una from the Saturdays and her needles in to my

house for the very last time, well the needles anyway, Una will come back

and check on me before I am released from the world of

chemotherapy.

So, today me, Nessa (BF) and the gorgeous Gaby went for the usual walk

in Attingham park, such a good start to the day with two of the best girls

and Saxon, of course. Then I headed off for lunch with the lovely

Christine which was   just perfect, making it a day with three of the best

girls. I am lucky. And pleased with myself, not sure I mentioned   that it's

a week tomorrow that I get to step out of this foggy, toxic world and back

into a real life one. The one I've been dreaming about for the whole of

this year.

That's a combination of having far too much time on my hands, having no brain to do anything overly constructive and desperately wanting to be well and whole and fixed and happy. There may be a bit more fixing to do, but I am getting super close to getting my world back. The foggy toxic stuff is not   welcome. Neither is the fear, that can go and take a running jump if it even tries to come anywhere near me.

So I am now doing the opposite of what I did at the start of this nightmare. I started by painting everything and making everything chemo proof to occupy my head to keep the fear at bay. I am now removing everything that reminds me of chemo and streamlining the house and all that lies within   it. Out with the old and all that. I'm being ruthless and I like it. This is also to keep me occupied, not from the fear but from being unbelievably bored of this. I still can't read, because of toxic stuff, and still struggle to hold any focus, but I am so bored of being in this suspended state.

Not long   now.

One-week tomorrow, have I said. To give me focus, I get to see James (MAB massive) tomorrow to start talking about going back to work, hallelujah!

So my rock and roll today has been full of three gorgeous

girls, walking until my muscles can't do it anymore and being very pleased with myself and what's happening one-   week tomorrow.

<u>26th September 2013</u>

One week today it will be done, over, finished, no more, not ever. I am of course talking about my chemotherapy. Not sure I've mentioned it, but it's only seven sleeps and I'm there!

So far, this countdown thing is going well. This time next week I'll be in bed feeling blooming awful but I'll be feeling blooming awful with a very big smile on my face, safe in the knowledge that I don't ever have to do the toxic stuff again. I very much like the sound of that.

So, my day started with the best man in my life, Saxon. Gorgeous Gaby was getting her hair done to make her more gorgeous, if that is in fact possible, so I took Saxon out for a couple of hours. I have to say he was very good company and was a dream to be with. He made me look like I knew what I was doing. I then headed off to see another man in my life, my boss of course, James. It's always a joy to see him, I love hearing what's going on in the outside working world and of course he keeps me on my toes, which is no bad thing.

However much I would like to go back to work as soon as possible, Mr. Sensible, and clearly Mr. Right, is being very practical about when I can actually go back, it may not be until January. Taking all things into account, the main one recovering from my surgery and getting rid of the foggy, toxic stuff, I have to make sure I am fixed and better before I'm allowed.

Something to do with having a life changing and potentially life threatening illness that makes it important, probably right. Maybe in

December I can start my phased return, who knows, but at least I know I'm in safe hands. Always nice.

Miss Daisy was having lots of fun at Beccy's house when I got back, as she always does, we love them and their open arms, we are lucky. Spelling practice, reading, showing off her new big tooth and second visit from the tooth fairy followed until she promptly fell asleep. I have to say I will not be far behind her. These 3-mile power walks maybe wearing me out, all for the right reasons, still not bad after 17 weeks of chemo! I am happily going to walk my way to next Thursday.

So, my rock and roll today has been all about hanging out with the boys, perfect.

27th September 2013

Less than a week to go. I shall never apologise for going on about this particular part of my life, you know, the bit about

nearly finishing chemotherapy. I know, its hard to believe I would 'go on' about anything.

Anyway, I love saying it, therefore I am. A lot. At every given opportunity. It feels mighty fine knowing that I am nearly on the other side of the toxic stuff. I am now officially in week 18.

That's week 18 of 18 weeks.

In your face chemotherapy - nearly. I also love the fact that other people are enjoying saying it too. I guess it is my favourite topic, but still, there is nothing better than hearing it or reading it. It makes me smile even more, if in fact that was possible.

So, I spent the morning trying to avoid all the Macmillan coffee mornings. Sounds bizarre that I would want to avoid them, given that they raise money to help people like   me. Next year I am sure I will be trying to get everyone I know to do something for it, but this year it feels far too close and I feel a little like people will be whispering and pointing - she's the one with cancer - type thing. I am very sure that is only in my head, but today I wasn't prepared to run the risk. I did manage to get to Beccy's just as it was finishing and no one was there. Perfect!

The rest of my day was even more perfect. Yesterday I got to hang out with the boys and today I got to hang out with the girls, of the best kind. It started with Miss Daisy, Scooby doo and spelling practice.

She is just like sunshine.

Then Gin Jayne, coffee and a very over due catch up. Much needed. Then the lovely Beccy, a walk and coffee and cake. Very tasty. Then the Gorgeous Gaby and Saxon, Attingham Park and our 3 miles. Perfect as always. Our walk was powered by much giddiness and realising that I've actually had a breakthrough of the emotional kind. Hallelujah!

Finishing back with Miss Daisy who is a true SWOT. Just like her Mum. I'm sure I was never this keen on homework though.

Not bad for 18 weeks of chemo. Eighteen weeks! I am out and doing woody woodland, deer park type walks and enjoying smiling more than I thought possible after 18 weeks of the toxic, foggy stuff. Amazing. I am also now tireder than a very tired thing.

So, my very excitable rock and roll today has been filled with the girls, breakthroughs, 6 more sleeps and smiling. But now this girl needs to sleep.

28th September 2013

So, as I sit at home pretending to be an X Factor judge with Nessa (BF) whilst she is in Leeds, trying to work out how we can share Gary Barlow and deciding on our girl band name for next year, I have realised that lots of little things happened today that I have been longing for. For about the last 18 weeks as it goes. Before I carry on, it is only right to mention that its five sleeps to the end of the toxic nonsense. This time next week I shall be partly comatose on the sofa watching X Factor feeling very smug and a little bit sick, no doubt, that it's done and dusted.

So, I started the day watching Strictly Come   Dancing. It wasn't watched last night as I fell asleep with Miss Daisy watching Scooby Doo in my bed at the ever so late time of 8pm. The crazy girl that I am. Not. Anyway, this reminded me of Christmas and I got that warm tingly feeling that Christmas isn't far, and that means that I am back, whole, fixed and well. I then sat on the gorgeous Gaby's sofa, a nice change from my own, and we were getting giddy about how we might be on Thursday.

I have longed to talk about the last one like its next week. It is now next week. That feels good. We were both a little taken a back that I'm nearly out of this bit, all that time that was stretching in front of me is now nearly over.

It is fair to say that I am unravelling a bit, in an emotional way, but a good way. All this adrenaline that has been holding me together. All my planning and all my strategies to get me through have worked. I am possibly letting myself see the bright lights of the finishing line and I am doing that thing you do when you first go on holiday, relax, and it all comes out. I shall hold it together until its done and then I need to let myself bask in the warm post chemo glow.

Whilst driving home, I realised it was getting dark at 7pm. Another thing I have longed for. I have been ill for three seasons and have been waiting for autumn, with all its colourful and dwindling day light glory to sprinkle it's end of chemo magic my way. By the time autumn is done, my treatment and fixing will be too. Woohoo!

So, its clear I watch too much TV at the moment. My strategy this week is to juice, eat, walk and sleep whilst hanging out with all the best people. TV happens when I am so tired I can't move. That happens a lot at the moment. I don't care as it's working. I also don't care how bad my taste in TV is, I am a lost cause on that front.

So, my rock and roll today has been all tingly and warm with only five days left of the toxic stuff and not long before I am whole, fixed, well and happy. Marvelous.

PS. I also wanted to find out who Larry is. Whoever he is, he is always happy. I wonder if he is as happy as me!

29th September 2013

So, it seems Larry and I have things in common. Thanks to the gorgeous Gaby, we now know that Larry, who is happy as Larry, is happy because he was a boxer from many moons ago. It seems he was very good, as no one could beat him. Lifting Gaby's words, this is very fitting for me. I am also winning all my fights with this nonsense, therefore I am also happy. As Larry. I may even be a little happier. I sure will be in a few days' time. Four sleeps and the toxic stuff can go and take a hike. Woohoo!

So, Miss Daisy heads off to party hard with her friends and to hang out with her Dad and I am left to my own devices. I have had a great day, organising, planning, getting excited, crying randomly but not in a sad way and generally getting myself ready for what can happen after four sleeps. Well, after a few more really due to the toxic stuff having an adverse affect on my health and well being, but, the best news is I won't ever have to do it again, so I can feel the adversity with a smile on my face. I am soon to be a well, whole, fixed and happy girl. Having won the battle of my life. Phew!

So, my rock and roll has been full of me being happier than Larry.

30th September 2013

Well, I don't think I had accounted for the emotion that being in the last week of chemotherapy brings. Not in a sad way. Far from it. In an unbelievable way. As in, I can't quite believe how I have got myself to only having three sleeps left. The girl that I can remember all that time ago, is not the girl who is walking her way to this Thursday.

So, I have spent today frantically getting ready, not really sure what for, apart from the obvious, of course. However, I have got myself ready for treatments six times over and it's never frantic. I feel like I am getting ready for something really big or I am pulling all the distraction tricks I can think of. My paint brushes even came out today, just so I could finish what I started all that time ago, as I sure as hell won't be doing any painting when I'm out of this nonsense. This worked as I was too busy to think about anything.

That all changed when I took myself off for a walk. Nothing like secluded woodland with random deer wandering around for me to start to think about why I have been feeling quite so at odds with everything. Of course I spent most of the walk crying, again not in a bad way and there was no one around, apart from deer and they kept their distance.

I actually can't believe its nearly over. This is a wonderful feeling and the tears are of disbelief, nothing more. The adrenaline that has kept me going through these 18 weeks specifically, but also from January really, is starting to turn into something different and I am allowing myself to feel. A bit like getting pins and needles when getting the feeling back in a dead arm or leg or something, my numbness is starting to lift and I am daring myself to feel what it might be like to be in the real world again. Everything I once took for granted has changed, I think I am starting to get my head around that now. It's only taken me nearly a year!

So, I walked, I painted, I organised and I dared myself to plan and of course I cried, a lot. I am now exhausted. Still not bad for 18 weeks of chemotherapy!

My rock and roll has been full of disbelief today, of the best kind, and of course only having three sleeps to getting rid of the toxic stuff once and for all.

<u>1st October 2013</u>

Hello October. How I have looked forward to welcoming you into my foggy world. October is the month that promises to bring some much needed magic my way, in the form of the very last blast of the toxic stuff.

So, after trying to work out why I was being chased by bears in my garden, I got out of bed and headed to the calendar. I turned the page with a smile that could light up the whole of the north of England, as I saw in very big letters 'LAST CHEMO EVER'. Joy, lots of joy, as in two sleeps time I shall be there.

So, in my world of foggy disbelief, I managed to watch a whole section of breakfast TV about breast cancer without running around the room singing to drown out the sound before I could find the remote to turn off. Progress.

I managed to render two people speechless. Not progress. Have a lovely lazy lunch with Catriona the magical cake baker and Zach. Perfect. And let Mary loose with her magical hands on my feet. Wonderful. No walking today on account of hardly being able to move from yesterday's outburst of distracted energy.

Apparently 18 weeks of chemo wares you out. I maybe feeling that today!

So, it's been a while since I have left anyone speechless, I sure hope that stops soon, its a little awkward. One was an estate agent lady asking me what the cold cap machine was and the other was a friend I bumped into that I hadn't seen for ages.

Very bizarre, I found myself trying to make light of it to break the awkwardness. It, being cancer. Not sure cancer can ever be made light of, but somehow I managed it, with a little help from Britney Spears. I have no idea if that's right or not, but it seemed to work in the moment.

Anyway, I am absolutely knackered, but I am feeling mighty pleased that it's pouring with rain, getting colder with the days are getting shorter and the Christmas decorations are in the shops. All this means I get to try out this new world I have in front of me. This is very exciting.

So, fingers crossed my blood is back to where it needs to be tomorrow when Una from the Saturdays and Celine Dion come and do all their tests. I sure hope it is, at this stage in the game I always worry about this. I know, me, worry,   never! I may have regenerated in every way possible, but I am allowed when it's this close to the finishing line.

So, my very tired and achy rock and roll today has been full of a lovely, lazy lunch, making progress and being in the magical month of October with only two more sleeps left of the toxic stuff.

Alex Jagger

So, big, massive curve ball. My blood is not alright. The test

that checks my immunity says its too low to have my treatment tomorrow. However, I am lucky enough to have Una from the Saturdays as my nurse and she is sure it is not right. I have no temperature, I look well, I feel well, she says it makes no sense. She is that sure she is coming to see me at 8am to take more blood and drive it to hospital and wait for the results. She is still convinced I will be having my treatment tomorrow. I hope she is right.

It takes everything I have to get through the treatment days. It's going to take all I have to get through a possible delay. I know I can't do anything about it and I know   it wouldn't be long before I can have it, but all the same, this is a bugger. I feel like I am falling at the final hurdle and that was not in any of my plans. I also know some plans are made to be broken, I just didn't want this to be one of them. What will be will be and all that. I am a little sick of saying that.

So, I have had the biggest glass of spirulina and all the rest of the green stuff and I have juiced all the fruit and veg I have in the house, for the second time today. I am going to have a bath and go to bed early and see if I can sleep.

So, there is no rock and roll right now, it's on hold. Fingers crossed it makes a return tomorrow.

3rd October 2013

Well, this was not how I planned today to go. Today should

have been the final day of 18 weeks of the toxic   nonsense. Instead it was
the day my body wasn't ready to be poisoned and the day I had to get my
head around being delayed for another week. I know it's only a week, to
most people, but to me this was the end of the hardest thing I have ever
had to do and the day that has kept me going through every one of those
18 weeks. A week in my world can seem much, much longer.

So, Una from The Saturdays came at 8am to take my blood, we both
cried, she left and I cried some   more. The gorgeous Gaby arrived, we
both cried. However, much logic either of us tried to apply to the
situation, it didn't take away that this felt a little cruel and we wondered
what lesson I had to learn, that I hadn't already. I really thought that as
life lessons go, I had leant the lot. Clearly not.

Una made the call, we both cried. Gaby had a good swear and I fell in to
utter disbelief. Again. I thought these days had gone, you know, the ones
that leave me speechless, empty, tired out, and full of pain. The feeling
you get when your heart is broken. Both of us felt it. Just rubbish. But, we
concluded that I had a choice. Get down and disillusioned or get back on
track with a new focus of next Thursday. The first one isn't an option and
as I am the master of picking myself up off the floor, I opted for the
getting back on track one.

Let the new count down begin. Seven sleeps.

Una did say that my blood count had risen from last night, but just not enough. But that's a good sign. The fact it's gone up and not down. This is just a blip and should be fine for next week. Fingers crossed. She also said that Mr. Blinky Eyes had said he was shocked this hadn't happened earlier in the treatment, on account of the amount of drugs I have had so far, super high dose and all that. Or 'intensive course of chemotherapy' as Dr Blinky Eyes calls it. I guess I need to be happy about that. I am.

So, I stick to Gaby like glue for a few hours, not sure what I would have done without her, and we go out for lunch and wander through the shops and the rain. Saxon got his first pair of shoes! I head off and buy Tesco's out of fruit and veg, as I intend to be the healthiest I have ever been, and decide to eat steak every day. Not a bad way to get those pesky white blood cells where they need to be, so I can finally kick chemo into touch. And anyway, we vowed to keep me very busy for this 19th week to make sure it fly's by. I wonder if my hair will start to grow back! I do still have what appears to be a full head of hair. Of course I know how much thinner it is so let's see if it makes a return in this 4th week. Whatever gets me through!

So, my rock and roll has been shaken but has resumed a reduced service today, however, it has been full of the very gorgeous Gaby for getting me through the day, Una from the

Saturdays caring enough to try, lots of people for some very lovely messages, steak and me being the master of getting myself off the floor, again. It's time for these white blood cells of mine to get a move on, they have seven days. And counting.

4th October 2013

It is not normal to long for the really sick feeling. However, this morning I woke up disappointed that, physically, I felt fine. Then it dawned on me why. Bugger. My body must go to a default setting when faced with bad news, that being uneasy, full of butterfly's and full of dread. That is how I felt this morning. My bad news this year has been of the big kind. The bad news yesterday was a mere set back, not news of the big kind and that is what I have been fighting against all day. I really need to move away from that default setting I have perfected, to something much more palatable.

So, I juiced, mixed, and drank all sorts of magical goodness and got myself out of the house, feeling like all I wanted to do was curl up in ball and cry. Luckily a quick visit from Dave got me out, preventing me from rocking back and forth on my own. The gorgeous Gaby, Saxon and Attingham park

then got me through the rest of the morning. By the end of our walk I was feeling much more like this was all doable and not the problem I had made in my head. For me, it was

disappointment of my worst kind, the suspended state of being and confusion at why my body didn't want to play. Something to do with lots of toxic stuff no doubt. All these worries and what if's are out of my control, therefore I have to leave them be. It is, what it is, because it is. (I now like that saying). All I can do is look after myself and send some goodness my way.

Anyway, Gaby helped me get over myself, she is very good at that. We had a good walk in the sunshine which is always good. Lucky girl that I am. I then headed off for coffee with the lovely Christine. Every Friday after my treatment Christine comes to see me for an hour or two, I have no idea what we talk about, or really for how long she is with me, but I love it as it's one of the hardest physical days in the treatment. As my treatment didn't happen, not sure I've mentioned that, I went to see her and this time I knew what we were talking about and all was good. And it got me through the afternoon. I also loved that. I just about did the school run without crying, a little touch and go but I made it out with the right child and no tears, from me.

So, safe within my own four walls with Miss Daisy, juicer on permanent juice mode, I vowed to have a week full of good people, walks, juice, green goodness, lots of super food, warm, relaxing baths and early nights. That sounds like the last 18 weeks. I need the next five days to be infection free

with the best blood count going and a head that is full of clarity and strength, not doubt and fog. If I get delayed again, so does my surgery, that I could do without.

So, I have rock and roll back again and it was full of the best girls, self preservation and juice. Lots of it. (and walnut whips minus the walnut!)

5th October 2013

It's hard work getting on top of the goodness factor, I have to say, but when it could mean the difference between kicking chemo into touch or having to wait another week, I think I will do anything to help my blood get itself back on top form. I really need to invent a juicer that cleans itself, even the guinea pigs are sick of the amount of juiced left over veg I'm trying to feed them.

Anyway, I've got my sparkle back. Still annoyed that I can't yet quote any Britney Spears songs and still worried that I may not be ready next week, if I'm not it won't be for the lack of effort on my part. Fruit and veg does not stand a chance in my house right now. I have this last year, but more

specifically the last 18 weeks, juiced a ridiculous amount of fruit and veg every day, along with a lot of green super food spirulina and wheatgrass type stuff that tastes absolutely horrible. I do believe this has played a part in getting me through the toxic stuff, that of the intensive variety, as well as

I have. But my poor body clearly needs a bit more, so its' wish is my command. 2013 will be known as the year fennel hit an all time high in Shropshire. It may seem I have a little fennel fetish. Bring on the time I can give it a miss and not feel I'm letting my body down.

So, my rock and roll today has been full fennel, fennel and more fennel, all drunk with a twinkle in my eye.

6th October 2013

So, I think I am the pied piper of all things fresh, green and wholesome, as it seems most of the vegetables for   the population of Shropshire are in my house. This juicing marathon I am on is tiring. Whatever gets me through to Thursday I guess. Who knew it would be such hard work to get a blood count back.

So, today I have been unbelievably tired and achy. I am not ill, apart from the obvious of course, I just think it's this fatigue thing that Mr. Blinky Eyes keeps talking about. I am, after all, on my 19th week of chemotherapy, its effect on my blood count has clearly left me a little worn out. I have been

in and out of bed like a yo yo, in between drinking vegetable juice and eating whatever I think will help me to get back on form. I am also in unchartered territory, you know, being in a fourth week of a treatment cycle. I am avidly analysing all

things me, to see if I start to get back to normal. Again, whatever gets me through, I need to get out more. It's only three more days of this mind numbing activity.

So, today my super tired rock and roll has been full of vegetables and sleep, all done with the twinkle in my eye still shining bright.

7th October 2013

So, today I continued my quest to break the world record for the amount of juiced vegetables one person can consume in any one day and the number of times one person can walk around Attingham Park in any one week. So far, I think I may be in for a shot.

So, my day went a little like this. Juiced veg, nasty green goodness drink, various other forms of natural stuff consumed, coffee with the lovely Christine (best bit of day), usual woodland walk, no crying, the deer were relieved, shops to buy more vegetables, bought Tesco out of fennel, again, then an evening with Miss Daisy being bossed around. You know, the usual.

Of course, I also had the joy of avidly checking for any signs of life on the hair growing front and the fascination of analysing all new 4th week changes in me. I feel much better than yesterday and am desperately hoping that I'm good to

go for Thursday or who knows what exciting things I'll get up to, I know, the anticipation is too much. Whatever gets me through to Thursday and all that.

So, my rock and roll has been full of a ridiculous amount of goodness, mind numbing ways to get to Thursday and being bossed around by the one and only Miss Daisy. No idea where she gets it from.

8th October 2013

So, here I am, still in the not so exciting world of waiting for the last session of the toxic stuff. Nervous as hell that my blood count won't be right for my blood test tomorrow, whilst trying to be philosophical that if it isn't, I just have to go with it. This week has been another little test for my patience and I am pleased to report that I think I have passed with flying colours. Another delay and I can't promise the same restraint and acceptance, but then again, I really have no choice. Tricky.

Anyway, me and the gorgeous Gaby made today, Specsavers day, as we both were there to sort out our eyes. I am the proud owner of some new glasses. Helps with the fog when I can actually see where I am going. I made my way to Mary

with her magical hands to sort out my feet and my back this time. I managed to stay awake so I could savior every last minute of the gloriousness. The rest of the day was taken up

with vegetables and being bossed around by Miss Daisy. Oh and the house fairies have made an appearance as I finally have a house viewing booked, hurray!

So, I am doing my best to be good to go for this week, I can sort of see me watching the first X factor live shows, feeling sick, (because of the toxic stuff, not the X factor, but then again!) with Nessa (BF) sitting on my sofa along with Gary Barlow. I am holding on to that image as it means I am done and dusted. Let's hope so, as analysing changes in the new 4th week of a treatment cycle, albeit fascinating for someone who really needs to get out more, is so very boring. Mind numbingly boring. My hair has started to grow back though, that kept me occupied for a while. Whatever gets me through - still.

So, my rock and roll has been full of the best girl with glasses, magical Mary, hopes for a perfect blood count and thoughts of Nessa and Gary Barlow keeping me company post the toxic nonsense.

9th October 2013

So, as Britney would say; 'hit me baby one more time'. I am good to go for my last ever chemotherapy   treatment. Hallelujah!

Dare I say I am actually excited to be having the toxic stuff tomorrow, you know the drugs, cold cap and the yucky

feelings after, but I can do it all with a smile on my face with the knowledge that I won't have to do it again. Ever.

So, today my day has gone a little like this: Miss Daisy's super cute assembly, blood being taken, having my phone glued to my side just in case I get my results, lovely visit from Nessa (sister) and Lou on their way to Scotland, keeping my phone glued to my side, lots of random furry animals, my   phone ringing and getting the best news. I get to finish chemotherapy and get the hell out of this horrible, suspended state of being which can make room for the start   of something wonderful.

So, Una from The Saturdays was overjoyed at my fantastic blood results, see, all that juicing must have paid off, and she arranged my morning treatment. Since then I have had the feeling of a 13-year-old girl on Christmas   Eve. Well, it's certainly not Christmas Day tomorrow, but it is the last day I will have to do this. EVER!

So, my very excited rock and roll has been full of Miss Daisy being super cute, unexpected lovely visits and having the best blood ever! Bring on the toxic stuff. The last one, not sure I've mentioned that.

10th October 2013

Well. I DID IT! It's done, over, finished, no more, never again.

I did it with the most amazing girl right by my side, the gorgeous Gaby of course, along with boxing gloves, real life ones, and a massive balloon. Perfect!

And of course Una from the Saturdays with her needles. If it hadn't of been for the toxic stuff and cold cap, dare I say I was enjoying myself.

So, it's time to let the relief sink in and to power on through this bit, the yucky bit. For the last time! EVER.

This girl now needs to be horizontal and sleep.

So my rock and roll has been filled with one of the best friends a girl can have, Una from the Saturdays and of course, me, for doing it! I believe that's pretty good rock and roll.

<u>12ᵗʰ October 2013</u>

So, my heart is full of happiness, the strangest happiness I think I ever felt. It is blatantly full of the sickly, tired happiness still, but happiness all the same. And that is, of course, because I have finally finished the toxic stuff. By far the hardest and longest part of this treatment and this journey, but now it is finally over. It hasn't quite sunk in yet, hence this strange happiness. I am sure 'strange' will turn into something quite wonderful very soon. Possibly when I stop feeling sick! I think I have only been happier the day Miss Daisy was born. New life and all that.

Finishing chemotherapy is momentous. The me that started sure isn't the me that finished. I think it will be difficult   for anyone to go through that and not change, but boy, have I faced some fierce demons. And come out on top. Which is the best bit. It took some doing, but I got there in the end.

So, its time for me to bask in the post chemo glow that I have been so waiting for.   This journey is not yet   over. I still have a mastectomy and reconstruction to come in four weeks' time and again in May. The reason I started to write this was to help me get through the 19 weeks of the toxic stuff. That worked. It gave me a focus, one that I sorely needed. It was also to be able to look back, if I ever wanted to, and for Daisy when she was older, if she ever wanted to know what it was all about.

So, for all those reasons I will carry on, albeit in less frequency. Let's face it, once I get my brain back, I don't have the excuse   of writing rubbish, so I best make sure its worth reading.

So, I can't finish this day

without saying the most massive of thank you's to anyone who has read this, at any time or all of the time. If it helps one person, it's been a good thing. It has helped me. A lot. I have had cancer, twice, six weeks of radiotherapy, nineteen weeks of chemotherapy, five surgeries this year so far with one big one looming on the horizon. Not sure I've mentioned all that before! It's been a hell of a year! Writing it all down meant I got it out of my head when it was happening, rather than it festering and turning into something bigger. Something that would turn out to be another juggernaut to breakdownsville. Been there the first time around and not intending on going back. Thankyou very much.

I could not have done it, as I have, without the thoughts and messages from people I know and don't know. And without the bestest of friends and family a girl could ever wish for. I may have been unlucky this year with the whole big C stuff, but boy, I am the luckiest girl when it come to friends, family and my very own Miss Daisy. And I have been the luckiest girl when it has come to my treatment and the wonderful angels that delivered it. Specifically, Una from the Saturdays, she is one in a million. Not sure how anyone can make you feel so at peace whilst being poisoned!

It was the treatment I feared the most. I feared what it would do to me physically and emotionally. It has done a lot. Killed cancer and changed me forever. In a good way, of course!

So, onwards and upwards as I have heard lots of the last 24 hours! It is my time to recover, and get my life back. I cannot blooming well wait! Let the happiness begin.

So, todays rock and roll is all about basking in my very own post chemo glow, recovering and being the happiest girl ever! With Nessa (BF) on my sofa.

ps. I kept my hair!

14th October 2013

So, I feel like I should be skipping through a field, the wind blowing in my hair, with the biggest twinkle in my eye, shouting at the top of my voice that I did it! Surely that's how you feel the minute the toxic nonsense is over? Well, partly. If I tried to skip anywhere right now there would be trouble. A 10-minute walk with Nessa yesterday put me in bed for an hour, so best keep the skipping to a minimum for now. I am skipping on the inside, even though I am not wholly convinced I am not getting poisoned in three weeks' time. I am sure this is normal.

So, I have been basking in my very own post chemo golden glow this weekend with Nessa (BF) on my sofa. Tired out, zapped from the inside out and feeling like I've done 10

rounds with Larry, the boxer who never loses, but happy, as Larry, in a very surreal way. Happy that today my cold cap machine left the house, It's served me well, but boy was I glad to see it go. Happy that my chemical romance was finally over. Happy that I can start having showers again over baths as I won't need to worry about my hair coming out. Happy that I can start to use nice smelling shampoo and conditioner. Happy I can use hair straighteners. Happy that I can wear perfume again. Happy that I can stop constantly seeing my hair flying off everywhere.

It is actually amazing I look like I have so much left! Happy that I get my veins back. Happy that I can plan. Anything. Happy that I can spend time with my favourite people without worrying where I am in a three weeks' cycle. Happy that I get Miss Daisy back to my normal days. Happy that I can talk about going back to work. Happy that I can finally think about what happens after October 2013. Hallelujah! Its fair to say. I am happy.

So, time to let the dust settle, for my post chemo glow to keep on glowing and for me to look forward to all the normal stuff. And the small matter of surgery in three weeks' time, but I'll think about that then.

So, my rock and roll today was all about little waves of pure excitement. Of the best kind.

20th October 2013

So, its been over a week since the toxic stuff. The last one. And everything is changing. My new life is unfolding right before my very own eyes and the possibilities feel endless. It is also super surreal. Momentary feelings of being trapped in the never endingness of treatment cycles wash over me every now and again, followed by the sort of relief I have never felt before. I want to tell whoever is standing near me that I have finished being poisoned, but believe that's a little odd. I somehow manage to refrain.

In my sleeping hours I dream that the police stop me to take my temperature and other such treatment related stuff. Of course I wake up and remember its over. It's a good feeling. More than good.

So, the things that have been making very happy are almost laughable. Prawns. I can eat prawns again. I love prawns! New shampoo and conditioner that smell beyond amazing, getting my hair cut, even more amazing. There are many more that I won't go into, but all these little things that never even crossed my mind before are making my feel the luckiest person in the world. I am, of course, still in my recovery bit, so can't get too carried away, but I am trying to change my routine so I can start to get my life back and put the most unbelievably hard 19 weeks of chemotherapy behind me. It's working. It will work even more when this stubborn fog lifts. Won't be long now.

So, I have been doing the usual obsessive healthy stuff to get through this bit and ready for surgery in a couple of weeks' time, you know, the juicing, walking and all the rest of it. I am no doubt stuck with being this healthy now, not sure anyone who has gone through the big C a couple of times can doing anything less than respect the body they occupy. I have it down to a fine art now though so all good. I am sure looking forward to drinking some wine though!

Anyway, I have also spent some great time with the gorgeous one, Gaby of course, Nessa (BF), Beccy and the lovely Christine, and a good first night out with the girlie girls, minus anything fizzy, but lots of Christmassy goodness. I could decorate my house now if I thought I could get away with it. Everything that glitters with Christmas cheer signifies the end to the illness that will have had me for 12 months. I may get a little carried away on the festive front this   year. Miss Daisy will love it. And on Miss Daisy, we have had some very good time together doing stuff I haven't done for 5 months. Perfect. I've even met with James from the MAB massive to get me back to work when I'm healed   from the slicing and dicing stuff.

This week I have my last ever tox visit with Una from   the Saturdays and my last appointment with Mr. Blinky   Eyes. I am not getting signed off as that takes years, but I am moving to just the one consultant, my surgeon. I was wondering if I

get a gold star, medal or some sort of certificate from Mr. Blinky Eyes on account of getting through something quite so barbaric. I believe I get my life. I am very happy about that. I may push for a well done sticker whilst I am there though.

So, my post chemo glow is as bright as ever and is making me one happy girl. I shall carry on getting used to the normal stuff and working my way through the process that is getting myself onwards and upwards. This I like.

So, my rock and roll is happy, toxic free and full of possibilities.

23th October 2013

So, here we go again. Time to get my head around the slicing and dicing. My post chemo glow has been interrupted by appointments and other such activities that are required to get me over the next hurdle. I have spent all morning in hospital being asked a million questions about my illness, and getting more confused about what is going to be happening on surgery day. I guess I have to trust that Dan the boob man and the lovely Mr. Usman know what they are doing.

Today, I wasn't convinced. Today I found out things I didn't know. Today I wanted my breast tissue gone. Turns out my breast tissue is pre cancerous. It really needs to go. And of course they know what they are doing, they just haven't

specifically decided what they were doing with me. Yet. I am in hospital for 4 nights, have a 7-hour surgery, and the end result will be fear free and will look glorious. That's all I need to know for now.

So, whilst sat in the hospital, the same hospital that delivered the cancer news to me twice, I realised that I have had one hell of a year. I realised when I rendered the nurse speechless whilst she was asking me the million questions, that I am mighty proud of myself for getting this far. For facing the darkest of the darkest demons and for getting through some harsh emotional times. Today I could have cried. A lot. I decided to meet the gorgeous one for coffee instead. That put me back where I needed to be. We laughed instead. All good. I realised that I still can't talk about cancer. Maybe I never will. Clearly I can still write about it though.

I am hoping that my meeting with Mr. Blinky   Eyes tomorrow doesn't have the same effect on me. I need to come out of that all guns a blazing as it should be my last one. I'm not holding out for my well done sticker. Una from the Saturdays gave me a box of hero's on Monday so that is good enough for me! I shall miss Una but will definitely keep in touch with her. I have spent the last few days getting rid of things that remind me of cancer, by smell or association. It has been very therapeutic.

Of course it doesn't involve people. It's the people that have got me to here. I couldn't be without the people.

Anyway, on a more pleasing note, I had my hair   cut. Fantastic! I have worn perfume and all manor   of wondrous things. I am frequently amazed that I am toxic no more. I have plans. I have a night in Leeds with Nessa and Abby, time away in Wales with the gorgeous one and then surgery. I have done my return to work plan that my doctor will either agree with or not tomorrow.

I can see the bright lights of life right in front of me. Just need to get through this last bit. Not long.

So my rock and roll today has been a little confusing and very enlightening. I believe I've done pretty well so far.

ps. A lovely night with Kate was perfect.

<u>24th October 2013</u>

So, the dust is settling, the relief is big and my emotions   are exhausting. The last 2 days have been full on hospital days with lots of talk of cancer. I don't like talking about it. I never will. But soon I wont have to. Hurray!

So, the day started at the doctors to get my back to work plan signed off. That was the easy bit. The genetic testing discussion was not. Of course I will have this test, it's all arranged now, but it breaks my heart to think Miss Daisy would have to go through anything like this. I know it would have broken my mums heart if she knew what was happening to me.

At least Miss Daisy gets the benefit of knowledge, and as knowledge is power, she can be prepared and take any necessary action needed when she's ready.   My head a little fried, I go to school and help walk   Miss Daisy's class to the Harvest Festival service at   church. How random! Daisy's teacher asked me if I would like to do it and of course I said yes. Miss Daisy was very excited, so much so she cried all the way there. She is so like her mother.

In church I had all on stopping myself from crying. Something happened to me in there that was very touching. I felt very lucky to be there, alive.

Church and   me don't really see eye to eye most of the time, but today we sure did. I managed to keep tear free. Good job or I doubt I would ever be asked to anything at school again.

Fresh from my warm and fuzzy moment in church I head to see Mr. Blinky Eyes. Even though I sort of knew this would be my last visit to see him, I was full of doubt. I guess that is normal. He was the nicest I have ever seen him, mainly because he was discharging me. I even made him laugh when I declared my need to never see him again. I am not discharged from my consultant, I won't be for years, but I am from Mr. Blinky Eyes. Hallelujah! I skipped out of his office, with both of us laughing. Who'd have thought he could laugh quite so much. No well done sticker in sight, but the laughing and not ever having to see him again worked   in compensation.

Every time I leave these oncology appointments I get in my car and cry. He was a fairly traumatic person to see. He   was, after all, the keeper of the toxic stuff and those   big decisions. Today was no exception. As I was waving bye bye to the one that blinks, I was sobbing my heart out in sheer disbelief that this bit was over. No more. Finished. This relief is so big sometimes I don't know how to handle it. Not a bad problem to have. Better than the ones I've conquered so far.

So, I am now exhausted. I need some light relief. Good job I'm heading to Leeds tomorrow to spend some time with Nessa and Abby, and then to Wales with the gorgeous one and our kids. I cannot blooming well wait.

So, my over emotional rock and roll today has been about bidding farewell to Mr. Blinky Eyes, warm fuzziness and ridiculously massive relief. This I like.

1st November 2013

So, it's November. This I am pleased about. It's taken it's time getting here, I can tell you this is the first time ever I have been happy about it being cold, rainy and the clocks changing. I am also mighty pleased about my 'best day ever' last week in Leeds that had been planned for months and my few days in Wales by the beach. The two things that have

kept me going at times. And of course I have been unbelievably pleased at the lack of the toxic stuff. There's a few things that have not been too pleasing though.

My blood is having s tough time recovering ready for next week, I have to have the scary surgery, the one I was hoping wasn't for me. Who was I kidding with my luck. And really unnecessary and stupidly upsetting issues involving insurance people. I doubt I have ever read any small print on anything and there was no chance I was going to start whilst having cancer. It's all sorted now. Turns out they needed to check their own small print before sending me scary bills.

So, yesterday would have been my treatment day, it felt good knowing it wasn't. That is where the goodness ended. I had frenzied calls from surgeons and hospitals with everyone panicking that my blood count was too low to do my surgery. Typical. I have had to come home early to get more blood tests done and am having more on Monday. Dan The Boob Man rang me expressing his concern. Just as I was relaxing in my post chemo glow, this happens as a little reminder that this is far from over.

So although I have maintained my healthiness, I have upped my game to get my blood good again. I am, again, at risk of causing a local vegetable shortage in Shropshire. I am also trying desperately hard not to worry. But, I am. I don't want

to have to go through getting new dates, more time with pre cancerous cells possibly lurking. I have my head around what is going to happen next, I now just want it to happen.

Anyway, it turns out it's quite tiring after 19 weeks of the toxic nonsense. My bones ache, if that's possible. I have also been relaxing into not having chemo again, something I have not done all year, which I am sure has the ability to knock anyone sideways after holding stuff together for such a long time. It's no bad thing. All I have to do now is consume vast amounts of goodness every day and get myself into hospital on Wednesday. How hard can that be!

So, I have had lots of rock and roll over the last few days but todays has been of the very tired and   juiced vegetable variety. Here we go again. This girl needs to sleep. Again.

3rd November 2013

So, whilst watching the X factor judges, judging whilst drunk it appeared,

I wondered if the joys of next weeks' show will be enjoyed from my hospital bed. How on earth X Factor has become the barometer to my illness and its progress, god only knows, but it seems it has. I am hoping that I will be, as that means it's done, one down, the blue one will be history.

I have had an odd day today. There have been many odd days throughout all of this, it has to be said. Odd days in the sense of dealing with the fear, the toxic stuff and losing my

way as well as my mind on occasion. Today, though, was different. Today was odd in dealing with the   relief. Knowing I am passed all of that, I've done the hardest bit and sometimes I can't believe it. Sometimes I don't know what to with this relief and sometimes it hits me that its been one hell of a year. And that is putting it mildly. I want to be normal, you know going to work, going out, talking about normal stuff, not thinking about big stuff, and I want to do all of that NOW! Of course I can't. I still have a date with Dan the boob man.

So, I have fulfilled my ambition of causing a national vegetable shortage in Shropshire this week. My juicer   is exhausted. If my blood isn't good enough   by tomorrow, it isn't anything I have done. Apart from have chemo of course. I am looking on the positive side and think I will be watching X Factor from hospital whilst nursing a fear free, fully reconstructed, me. Well nearly anyway, I'll be   half way there.

So, I'm off for more blood tests in the morning. Let's hope its good news. Bizarre that going into hospital is good   news. How things have changed!

So, my rock and roll today has been odd, full of anticipation and vegetables.

5th November 2013

So, my date with Dan the Boob man is on. The next leg of my journey is about to commence. Next stop, the nearly done town, very close to the city of getting your life   back. Hallelujah! I have wanted to explore that city for so long. I have more than got my head around this. I have my pi's packed and am ready to rock and roll my way to new boobs, the fear free kind. Well, one of them anyway, for now. But, this time tomorrow, my treatment for cancer will nearly be over. How good does that sound.

So, everyone in Shropshire can start buying vegetables again, fennel will no longer be sold out at Tesco's as my juicer will be having a few days' break. Clearly my plan worked as my blood was fine again. It is a good thing that I respond so well to all this juicy goodness.   I feel bizarrely fine about tomorrow, excited even to be getting this bit done. That may change in the morning, but for now, I feel good. On Friday, not only will it just be about recovery, I will be in unchartered territory as it will be he fifth week since the toxic stuff. That's exciting in   itself!

My hair is already growing back, the fog is lifting a little in my head and I feel that every day I can do something new. This is the sort of stuff that is good news for me right now, however small it seems, it means I am coming back to life.

So, whilst the rest of the country is oohing and aching at fireworks in the sky, and Miss Daisy is flying around on roller coasters, I am getting in the surgery zone, packing, cleaning and tidying and generally making sure all is good. I have to remind myself I am not actually going on holiday, but going into hospital. Trust me, I am not excited about the slicing and dicing stuff, I am waiting for the relief of it being done.

So, my rock and roll is all about bidding farewell to the blue one. My surgery awaits.

10th November 2013

So, I am declaring, wholeheartedly, that I have exceeded my own good nature. Everyone has a limit to what they can handle at times. I have now exceeded mine. And some.

It is very true that I have held myself together with a fine piece of thread on occasion, to get through the last few months, nearly a year to be more precise. Adrenaline is an amazing thing. It has kept the wolves from my emotional door and the energy stealing fairies well and truly away from me. No doubt they are hanging out with the house fairies, playing a very good game of hide and seek. But the energy stealing fairies have now done their best with me and the wolves have torn the flesh from my very weary bones.

It is also true that I have just finished 19 weeks of the toxic stuff and have just had major surgery. I clearly thought I was the expert at operations having had five so far this year.

They were small, very significant, but small in comparison. How wrong was I. I have just been in surgery for the same amount of time that Miss Daisy was in school and I can declare that I now have nothing. Nothing at all. Apart from my emotions and an unbelievable amount of pain. But I guess that's what happens.

So, it's not from the lack of people around me. I think the hospital needs a new visitors book after my stint here I have had so many visitors. Perfect. It's not from the knowledge I am nearing the end of this nightmare, because I am. Even with my surgeon yesterday freaking me out at having to wait for yet more results. Poor man. I cried so much declaring to him that I had nothing left to deal with anything, that he awkwardly put his hand on my shoulder apologizing. He sent Wendy his breast care nurse later to check he hadn't totally devastated me. I cried all over her as well. In fact I have cried at everything over the last two days and I feel like I don't know how to stop.

I don't feel safe yet. I thought I did. I don't. Not sure why, maybe as last time my treatment was over I found more cancer. I need to get over that. Maybe now I know I have more results nothing will change until after them. Maybe I need to allow myself to accept that I have just gone through something that I wouldn't have said was humanly possible. Maybe it's the chemicals making their way out of me causing havoc with my head and ability to see clearly. Maybe it's my lack of juicing! Maybe I am just too tired out.
So, I'm done for a while. There is no glow, peace, or contentment just yet. Instead, there are drains, dressings and absolutely no energy.
My rock and roll is asleep and nursing an emotional overload. I'm sure it will be back soon.

Ps. If anyone ever tells you it does not hurt removing drains, they are lying. I just practically passed out with it.

11th November 2013

I'm home, hallelujah! New boob, bandages, drains and a whole lot of pain. I may have been a tad naive about how I thought I was going to get through the last few days, to how I actually have. I am not going to post what I actually wrote yesterday (I did in the end) for this blog as it made me cry today when I re read it. I'll just say, the last few days have been unbelievable hard. Yesterday I exceeded my own very good nature. Yesterday I had a shiny first class ticket back   to breakdownsville. Everything that has happened over the last 12 months ravaged me, uncontrollably and unbelievably.

My heart felt like it was breaking all over again. I was sure I would feel fear free and safe. I don't. Yet. But, as soon as I got home, my troubles lifted. Miss Daisy had arranged pink balloons for me with Nessa and Dave, along with Yorkshire puddings and gravy and all my favourite food. All goodness was resumed.

So, apart from the emotional stuff, all went well with my surgery. The hospital now needs another visitors book after my stint with the amount of super splendid people that came to see me. Perfect! And with the emotional stuff, I have come back around to knowing that such big surgery is tough, especially after 19 weeks of the toxic stuff, so I have given my self a break.

I am so tough on myself, it is true, on this occasion I am giving in. I have nothing left. Nothing. I have to go with the fact that everyday I will get stronger, but for now, I got nothing. I am smiling again though.

So, me and my drain are propped up, not doing much apart from getting better. That will do for now. I have lots of people popping by which is just perfect. I can share my very interesting hair stories, well, about my own hair, growing back like wild fire. Hurrah! I better change my chat or I may end up lonely!

So, my rock and roll today is in slow motion and is very ouchy. For now.

12th November 2013

So, I can safely say this surgery has well and truly stopped me in my tracks. It's obvious why. I have been reconstructed. I

wonder if this is how the bionic woman felt (if there was one) and I wonder if I will be bionic. Anyway, this pesky drain follows me around, it really isn't normal to have a tube popping out of my back. It is not conducive for a good night's sleep, or anything really. Having my back and front bandaged up is a bit of a bugger. I have had a muscle removed from my back and had a skin graft and the front, well it's the   front. I can't really see what it looks like yet on account of all the swelling and the fear of looking at the blooming drain. Such a woos!

So, incapable of being able to do very much for my self which is mighty frustrating, gin Jayne came with her meals on wheels and she took me for a walk in my garden. First fresh air for nearly a week, lovely. Miss Daisy also came with her noodles for tea. Those were my highlights of the day. The rest of the day I did a little too much thinking, oh no!

I had a little contemplation about this time last year. Nothing is the same. What a difference a year makes. Gin Jayne nailed it earlier by telling me I was probably in shock. I agreed as it does explain my over emotional and rather empty state. Oh boy, I quiver at the thought of what I have been through. I have no idea how I have got here. But I have. With a little help (big help) from my friends I guess.

So, the twinkles in my eye and the ideas in my head back in November 2012 are no more. Some of that is sad, some not

so, some I miss, some not so. Regardless of how I feel about a year ago, it's gone. What has followed, well, that's been pretty life changing. I sometimes get very strong yearnings to be back in November 2012, in ignorant bliss. But that's just silly.

Time to get my twinkle back and get moving with any crazy notions I have been cooking up. When I can move that is. I just need this bit of time to accept what's happened to me and then to put it away. Probably when I get the results from my surgery next week, which hopefully will be good, will I be able to move on up.

So, my rock and roll today has been full of ouchy contemplation and meals on wheels from the gin lady.

14th November 2013

So, here I am in my 6th week post the toxic stuff, drain and bandage free.

Yesterday I was with Dan the boob man who was mighty impressed with my progress. I stood with him in front of the mirror viewing my many stitches all around my back and front when all my dressings had come off and maybe I could have been a little shocked. What I was, for the first time, was calm and happy and fairly impressed. I could almost say I was feeling a little peace with what has been going on and dare I say I even felt a little safe through my very emotional ouchiness He was very happy with his work.

Every cloud and all that. I maybe forming somewhat of a crush on him. Must be something to do with the amount of time I spend with him without my top on!

So, the whole drain thing took me surprise. No-one had prepared me for those, or how unbelievably painful it would be having them taken out. I almost passed out with the first one and I have a seriously high pain threshold. Not having them has been wonderful. There is nothing natural about having a piece of plastic tubing poking out of your back, I can tell you.

But, eight days on from my surgery, I am off pain killers just about and doing my best to move nice and gently. The best bit is I can have baths, showers, wash my hair as often as I like, use nice smelling stuff and the list goes on. All the stuff that means nothing to anyone else, means so much to me. I also shaved my legs today for the first time in 5 months, yippee! I do like it when my body responds well, you know, hair growing back, new boob, no longer blue, healing well. It means all is well with me.

Anyway, I shall carry on healing and looking after my bruised and swollen self. I have well and truly given in to this, it seems it has been the only way.

So, my rock and roll is still very ouchy but is certainly full healing goodness.

20th November 2013

So, here I am, two weeks away from the start of all this crazy cancer stuff last year. That is more or less one whole year, 365 days of utter nonsense. And today, I was told the great news that my mastectomy was a success with no cancer lurking. That kind of means I am cancer free. I like how that sounds. Of course I don't get any such grand statements of being all clear, that is a few years away, but we all have to start somewhere and I think this is a pretty good place to start for me.

So, it's time to finally live without the fear. That means saying goodbye to this diary. I started writing it to give me focus through the bad toxic days and to get me through the 19 weeks of dread, oh and to stop me from online shopping. It worked, apart from the online shopping bit of course. Well, come on!

It has, at times saved my sanity, allowed me to venture to my darkest depths and has given me the focus I needed to get me through the day. I hadn't accounted for quite so many people reading it. That helped me more than I knew and the messages I had at random times saved me. It has been as big a part of my illness as the toxic stuff. A much less invasive part, it has to be said, but a part all the same. It's now time to relegate it to my past along with the cancer, radiotherapy, countless surgeries and the toxic nonsense. I need start living this oh so precious life of mine.

So, here goes.

The girl writing this now is different to the one that was facing fear in its very ugly face all that time ago. I   still face that fear every now and again, maybe I always will, who knows, but logic says that all will be good with me. I doubt anyone who has gone through this can be the same person that started out. All those weeks of the toxic stuff does something, apart from kill cancer. It touches the very depths of your soul, shifting perspectives and forcing demons into places they were never allowed to venture in the past.

I may not have handled everything well at times, but handled stuff I did. I look back now, 7 weeks after my treatment, 2 weeks after my surgery and 1 whole year of having cancer, in utter astonishment and a whole lot of shock.

I did it. I got through every single thing that was put in front of me.

I had no idea I had it in me. At times I have wished I could have changed how I handled stuff. It turns out I was too far gone in the depths of despair to handle anything with any rationality, so that I will have to settle with. But, I think I was allowed to lose my mind when faced with that kind of recurrent fear, even my consultant had a tear in his eye today talking about it. That ability to make grown men cry again! But of course, if I'm going for wishes, it would be never to have had cancer in the first place. Obviously.

So I am, fundamentally still me. I am hoping I kept the good bits anyway. These last 12 months have taught me many things and I have, a million times over, vowed to be true to myself, not to regret anything, live every second with love in my heart and laugh. A lot. Oh and not to be so blooming neurotic. I know. Hard to believe! There is no way I can go through this most challenging of times and not come out the other end smiling. That bit was sort of non negotiable.

So, along with my own fear facing, demon conquering activities, I could not have got through this without all the amazing people around me. Those near and far, those I know well and those not so well, everyone has played a part in saving me more times than anyone ever knew. The ones that have walked and talked with me, got me through my treatment days, travelled miles to see me, went on actual roller coasters with me, made me laugh and sat with me when I could hardly move. Those that helped keep Miss Daisy smiling. The amazing nurses with amazing names who poisoned me, for all the right reasons, the clever clogs specialists who fixed me. Those who have taken the time to read my story and come on my journey with me, those who drank coffee with me, gin with me, those that celebrated my milestones, held their breath for me at times when results loomed, those that have truly loved me.

All these things have been, not only heart warming, but truly healing. For that I say the sincerest thank you I could possibly say.

These truly wonderful people have listened to me obsess about my hair, hair loss, hair thinning, hair colour, you name it when it came to my hair. (I kept enough to get away with it, phew!) They have listened to me bargain with time, they have seen me walk my way through the toxic stuff, juice more vegetables than is humanly possible, drink all manor of potions in an attempt to protect my blood and my veins, have picked me up when the fear took hold, have watched the worst TV with me known to man, over and over again, have not told me how ill I looked towards the end of the toxic nonsense until I looked better again and have just been there, whenever I have needed or wanted. A girl cannot ask for much more than that.

I am now so very happy to be able to say that I am fixed, healed, and more than ready to live my life with everything I have. I will feel the elation that everyone promises, for now I am cautiously relieved and a little full of disbelief that it is actually over. My heart was broken into a million pieces by the disease that I feared the most. With the help of those that make me the luckiest girl around, my heart feels almost whole again. If the gorgeous one and the girl from Leeds had charged for their time, they would be millionaires!

And of course there is Miss Daisy. The girl I wanted to live for, the girl that brought back the twinkle in my eye and the girl who remains as happy as me. I said at the beginning, life for her did not work without me. The thought of her not having me was a thought too far. She has tackled this year with laughter and tears, but mainly laughter. Luckily she is on top of   the world and has kept smiling the biggest brightest   smile. Like mother like daughter.

So, to everyone who has been by my side or been on my ridiculous ride from a distance, thank you. I raise my glass to you. It is now time for to me to change the world in my own, healthy, way. And finally, work beckons! I cannot wait. In a couple of weeks, I will be back, raring to go on my phased return. If, in fact, you can be raring on anything that's phased, but I will try.

So, my rock and roll today and every day, is all about whole heartedly giving it everything I've got. Adventure is waiting.

Alex Jagger

23rd February 2014

So, I'm back!

Fast forward 3 months from where I left off, in fact when I said my big thank you's to all the amazing people as I needed bask in my post chemo and surgery afterglow - safe in the knowledge the worst bit was over. I needed to go and live this new life I'd imagined I would have after going through such a traumatic year.

Well, it turns out I am not super human. This is the time that people don't talk about, the aftermath of cancer and chemotherapy, the dreaded toxic stuff, the stuff that touches the very depths of your soul, shifts perspectives and changes absolutely everything. The toxic warnings on the side of the box that the chemo drugs come in, need to have a second health warning...' kills more than cancer... changes your whole damn view on the world. What you once believed to be true no longer resonates. What was once you, no longer is and the chance to live is, at times, strangely and wonderfully overwhelming. Deal with it how you see fit.'

I happened to mention to Nessa (BF) tonight that I wished a little that I had kept my journal going as the last few months have been super hard in a very different way than before. She said it was my responsibility to write about

it.... So, here I am! I have Nessa to thank for getting this onto paper and for ultimately helping me to deal with what has been and what is to come.

So, everyday I find myself searching for my new   normal. What is it and what the bloody hell have I done with it? I have absolutely no idea anymore. I have no idea how to handle how I feel. Firstly, this is not a sad time. Quite the opposite. I am wonderfully happy and at times unbelievably sad. Maybe we all are. I want to scream from the highest mountain that I am well and truly alive. I want to run as fast as I can, which actually is not fast at all right now, but you know what I mean. I want to start doing all the things   I promised to myself in those dark toxic days.

And on occasion I am scared that the fear will never leave me. It still gives me sleepless nights. It still makes me want to cry when I look at Miss Daisy and the thought that she could have been motherless so young. It makes me feel like I am just like my own mother. I, of course, have no idea if I am on account of her popping her clogs far too early in my life, not to mention in her own life, but like her on the cancer front. So far I am. I am very determined, however, to leave the cancer similarity there.

So, the last three months have been interesting. It is four months after my chemo and three months after my

mastectomy. I have gone back to work...yeah! It is true to say that I love my job and as soon as I stop being the girl who's had cancer, the better!

They say there's only one thing worse than being talked about and that's not being talked about – I am being talked about a lot. I look different and I think it blatantly obvious that I am trying to fit into my old, comfy pair of shoes that was my life and they hurt like hell. For someone who loves a good pair of shoes, I'll be damned if I can find a pair that fit this new me.

I have been tired and have realised that my brain is not back to firing on all cylinders just yet. Damn chemo brain, it takes time for the fog to lift. But lifting it is. I have realised that my body is quite weak, from the inside of my bones out. In fact, my body is completely different. I look different and feel different. I've developed a massive dislike to juicing, painting, anything in fact I did through the toxic stuff. I feel unbelievably sick when faced with any of those things. Annoying really. I am sure it will pass.

I still want to cover my eyes and ears at every single cancer   advert, maybe I always will. Just as I get a shudder through the whole of my body when I hear about someone losing their battle with cancer, that stops me in my tracks but makes me feel lucky and scared at the same time.

My hair, now I can talk about this with true passion! My obsession with my hair continues. It is growing back curly. I had no idea how much I had lost until it started to grow back. Boy, have I got hair! It is not as it was and I believe it never will be, but that is what this is all about. Nothing is as it was and I believe it never will be.   Now, this is not a bad thing. Not sure how I feel about my curly hair, but mini straighteners do the job and Dan the boob man sure worked his magic on me. When the magic is done, I will be safe. Every cloud and all that. The big bit. This is my one and only chance to create my new future. That has to be a good thing. So, why is this not sitting right with me yet? Why am I in a pickle about most things one minute but gloriously in control of my future the next? I believe this is called the cancer effect.

What to do! Well, this is what I am doing. I am writing about it again. I am saying in a big loud voice, never underestimate the post cancer effect and all that it brings. Each person gets through this nonsense in their own way. This is mine, along with my super amazing friends and my very own Miss Daisy that is. Oh and I bought my own house, the one I was already living in! I'd like to paint it but can't on account if it making me feel sick. Bummer!

So, this is it. This is my story. The story that began with cancer, fear and an awful lot of the toxic stuff. The story that moved on to the sheer joy of getting through it with a new found love for a new found life. The story that now continues, full of possibilities. Full of the unknown and in search of what all this means. Physically and emotionally, how the hell do you keep yourself smiling and mean it after all this nonsense. Well, I'm about to find out.

So, my rock and roll today is all about Nessa, a phone call and this post. I'm checking in on what happens when the dust supposedly settles. I'm going in search of my new life, for the shoes that fit this girl that's writing this now, not the girl who has written every word before. That girl is still me. I need new shoes.

5th May 2014

Hello again. Three months have passed. The dust has far from settled. I still can't find my new shoes.

I told a story, a real life, true as could be, straight from the heart story. It was my story, you know the one about a whole lot of cancer, chemo and slicing and dicing and everything else that went along with it and a few things that didn't. I thought I had said everything I needed to about that story. I thought I was done. I had said all my thank you's, tried really hard to find that feeling of elation that I was sure was going to happen and had promised to live life with all of my heart. I was a little hasty. Not about the living life bit, the other stuff. I was too quick to run back to a world I thought I could just join and take up where I left off.

I was too desperate to try and pretend nothing had happened to me, with the need to be 'normal' again being so strong that I fled, ran for the hills, not knowing actually how tricky it was going to be. At that time, I naively thought that meant just getting back to work. Oh how wrong I was!

That is almost laughable now. This has been the most challenging six months for completely different reasons.

Now, don't get me wrong, these months have been, well, interesting, but more on that later. The reason I am telling

this story again is that it's time for the final chapter. It is of course, my last mastectomy and reconstruction. The last piece of the jigsaw, the end of my treatment. I didn't realise how important it would be to tell the whole story, for all the reasons I started writing it in the first place.

For the purely selfish reasons of getting me through, it is amazing how much a focus this can be when the rest of the cancer world is going mad around me. Since getting my date last week, I have been thrown back into a world I thought I had left behind. Telling my story clearly gets me through. For Miss Daisy, just in case she ever wants to read about how we did it.

The wonder of Miss Daisy, she knows far too much about cancer for a 6-year-old. Sometimes she hugs me so tight and asks me how my boobs are. As you do! And for the people that have read this, the many, many people, you have warmed my heart. A lot. For that reason alone, I want to tell the whole story.

So, I'm on the countdown for surgery. Three weeks and two days. It's that blooming 3-week thing again! Anyway, turns out it's big surgery, I sure played that down last year. I play things down for my own benefit and that of Miss Daisy. Not because I want to appear hard as nails or stronger than superwoman. It's all for self preservation and protection.

'Yeah I'm fine thanks' has become my favourite answer to anything to do with me. At times I have even made out all was well. I vividly remember speaking on the phone on New Years Day, the day before I went back to work and the day before the anniversary of me being diagnosed for the first time saying how great I was, trying desperately to come across as being well, happy and fully in control of all my faculties. I, of course was telling fibs, mainly to myself as I was breaking inside. Crazy talk.

I needed to play everything down so I could appear to be 'normal'. Almost like it never happened. I have since learnt that this will always be a part of my history. It certainly doesn't define me and I don't feel the need to talk about it, she says writing instead, but I will never hide away from the fact that this has been hard with a capital 'H' and I am mighty proud of me, for getting myself to the here and now.

So, the last 6 months. This is the stuff that no one talks about. Maybe because if someone did tell me I had another 6 months of pain to get through, it would have been too   much. I may have caused bodily harm to anyone who   even went there with that type of conversation. Maybe we are all different and maybe some people come out of this and just get on with life as it was. Not me. Of course. I guess there is no surprise there.

So, I went back to work in January on a phased return. I

tried very hard not to take it personally that three of my line managers resigned in the first three months. I am blessed with a fantastic team of people to work with and I have loved every minute of getting back into it and feeling my brain come back to life and feeling my chemo brain disappear. The joy of being able to think and talk about anything other than cancer was refreshing, a joy that I still revel in.

I got back to full time in March, and even though I still have hard days when it comes to me, I feel unbelievably grateful for a great job that takes me out of myself enough to push on through. That's been the easy part, I'm a geek when it comes to work as I actually love it, I want to change the world, remember.

Physically I am not the girl I was. For obvious, reconstructed reasons, and for even more obvious chemo reasons. Everyone said that recovering from chemo takes months even   years. Never, I thought. That will teach me to be pig headed. I am still recovering from the first surgery, that was 6 months ago. I spent Christmas with a black eye, every tiny trip or bump ends up in big bodily destruction, And I spent the whole of January and February in bed by 9pm. Who am I kidding, I sleep at any given opportunity. Even in nightclubs, it turns out. And I wonder why I am single! (I am by choice, not by serial nightclub napping by the way).

Anyway, to counteract all of this physical nonsense I am back

on the super juicing, I had a minor self rebellion on that front for a while, but I got over myself and found my way through, and I'm seeing a personal trainer to get fit again. Yes, I am paying someone to make me feel like I'm going to pass out on a weekly basis.

You will be pleased to know the obsession with my hair is still going strong. Not about how much I am losing this time, more like how curly it is getting. It is thick and curly, very curly, with a life of its own. I am lucky that it has grown back so strong and healthy, the jury is out on my curls. I say that. At times it knocks my confidence in the biggest   way. People comment on my hair all the time, they must genuinely like it, or why else would anyone comment on it, not knowing my past. I have a horrible habit of saying, 'oh thanks, but I had chemo and its grown back this way'. Talk about a conversation stopper. I really need to stop that; my hair is my hair. One thing I know; it will never be the same.

And there it is.

Nothing will ever be the same. And there lies the emotional 'ness of all of this. This is what I have been wrestling with. Now, I'm not saying that is all bad, but it sure is tricky. What was normal before all this, is not now. How I used to react to

things then, is not how I feel happy doing so now. How I thought about things then, is not how I do now. In fact, I went through a few months of having no idea how to think about things, how to react to things and therefore didn't do so very well. I didn't know what I needed or wanted. Confused and emotional summed me up for a few weeks. I couldn't see the bigger picture, I could only see what had been and that is no place to get stuck. Those who got me, saw past my confusion, those who didn't, well, just didn't get me. I have these angels that I call my friends who fly in and rescue me, whether they know it or not, but that has always been the case. Lucky girl that I am.

So, normal has changed because I have. And this is now the exciting part. I think. The uneasiness of being back in this world, the one I have been trying so hard to escape, is making me look back through different eyes. Now I am seeing the bigger picture. I am getting myself unstuck from the past as I can see an end to my treatment, that being my surgery. I can almost sense that the feeling of elation, I keep going on about, is not as far away as maybe it once was. I am saying that with caution. The elation of the past overwhelmed me so much it turned into confusion about who I was, what made me happy, what I thought about most things – you get the picture.

I am looking forward to telling my story right to the bit where I don't need to tell it anymore, when it's all done and dusted and all a part of my history, you know the one that has made me who I am today. All curly haired, a little confused, but very willing to discover what can be.

Memory is a powerful thing. When times are tough, memories hide, a coping mechanism I think. But these memories come back with a little effort. Due to my current countdown I am summoning my memories about what's to come. So far, my biggest distress is that I'm going to have to find a handbag with handles not straps as I won't be able to have anything on either shoulder or across my body. Now, talk about getting my priorities right... not much change there then! Let the countdown begin.....

26th May 2014

So, where to begin. At the beginning I guess could be a good place. Not on this occasion. We all know what went on back then and I have no desire to head back that way, so how about the beginning of where I left off in November. That seems like such a long time ago. Last year I spent time bargaining with time. Finding ways to make it go quicker, willing it to pass so the pain I was feeling would go.

This year, time has flown by, as it does. But for me to look back now, to then... WOW... is all I can say. What a journey I have been / still on. The best bit? This journey is coming to a close. I have, maybe had, become stuck in the past. To become unstuck was the tricky part, and this is the stuff that no one talks about. When the world of treatment stops, all the medical people go, all the nurses that I saw every 2 weeks stop coming and everyone who has been there, takes a step back. For all the right reasons. Things change.

Me being me, I wanted all this to happen quickly, to jump back into a 'normal' world. I even talked about going back to work 5 weeks after my surgery I was so desperate to get back to life, thankfully I was talked out of it. I waited at least 6 weeks. It was a time when I was not 'doing' anything.

And there lies one of the problems. I am a doer. If I am 'doing' I am distracted enough from what is actually happening and I can get on and forget.   Throughout the toxic stuff I was doing it, I was living in 3 weekly cycles and every day I had a focus and a plan to get through each and every minute. For surgery I was too ill to be bothered, and too drugged up to be fair. No bad thing. But when all the drugs wore off and the drains were out and I was just recovering, this thing happened.

Thinking.

Oh, it's a bugger at times. Just when you thought you were doing good, all those pesky feeling and emotions of what has happened come flooding back and the fear or what to do next takes hold. A completely different kind of fear to the one

I have been used to. This wasn't a cancer fear; it was a post cancer fear. I didn't even think that existed. I have to say I felt really guilty at times. Guilty that I wasn't swinging from the tree tops in utter elation. After all, I was alive wasn't I. I did not feel that at all. I felt wounded, vulnerable and exposed and knackered, absolutely knackered. I had been in a bubble for 12 months, a cancer bubble it has to be said, but a bubble all the same. Without realising it I had protected myself from the outside world and had only allowed those people near me who I trusted and who kept me going in that bubble.

Again, me being me, I decided to burst that little bubble of mine far too quickly. I didn't understand why I was being told to slow down, watch myself, don't rush back to work, take time to recover. In my head all I could think was, all I had been dong was taking time to recover, I'd had enough of taking time. In fact, all I had being doing was wrestling with time, why on earth would I want to take more time. Well. Hindsight is a wonderful thing. Bursting my bubble so prematurely left me even more wounded, vulnerable and exposed. And very sensitive to pretty much anything. Not how I had envisaged the end of my chemo, I have to say. It is only looking back that I can see this. I would have vehemently denied any of this a few weeks ago. All of my feelings, moods and randomness now make perfect sense. At the time I couldn't understand what the bloody hell was wrong with me.

So, how to get past all of this. Well, I have to do it on my own. Well, actually with a little help from my friends, unknowingly mainly on their part and a host of other people thrown in for good measure. I'm not that stupid!

I don't need counselling. I can tell you now, I'm in a pickle due to having had breast cancer – twice and all that. I need someone who can look past cancer and see me – for me. The strong professional woman, mother, friend and all out good person, not a victim to circumstance. Serendipity played a blinder and I found a coach and mentor to make me work for my bright future.

It has to come from within me, I have to really feel this to believe how far I have come. And there lies another tricky part! Never ending this! I know I am the queen of picking myself up and getting myself back to something. I've been doing that for well over a year. This time I don't want it to be just 'something'. I don't want to fall back into the same old, same old 'something' that was.

This is the really important bit. The bit that has had me in a pickle.   I can't go back and be that girl. I can't just go for same old, same old 'something'. I am discovering what my more than 'something' actually means.

Now, that's what I call an adventure, one which I have only just discovered as an adventure. It was a pickle just a matter of weeks ago.

The gorgeous one often says to me that things have to really hurt for you to take enough notice of them, to actually   do something about them. If things are just an annoyance or a bit of a nuisance, then they can pass you by and you may never do anything about them. When everything hurts, really hurts, it's time to sit up and listen.

Well, I am well and truly sitting up, standing actually, and listening like I have a million hearing aids in my ears. Listening to demons that   I thought were well departed, to fears that I had kept well hidden and to myself. These are new demons, not the ones I fought off through chemo, these ones were clearly immune.

Finally, I am listening to myself. How crazy is that.   I did a pretty good job of not believing I was enough. Not trusting my own instincts to find my new and improved 'something' for myself. It turns out I am enough, for   me. Turns out I have everything I need right in front of me. And that new and improved 'something' that I'm after is right there, ready for the taking. It is more about what I want, because I have a choice about pretty much anything I want to have a choice about. Sounds very simple, but, trust me, this is very liberating for someone who has walked in my shoes for the last 18 months. I do have a good shoe collection, but even a good pair of Jimmy Choos wouldn't be enough to walk back

in those footsteps. Those shadows of past thoughts and beliefs that try to come and trick me, are just   that. Shadows. No way the real thing anymore.

And that's it, right there. Progress.

Oh, and I believe I have resolved my bag situation. I have a bag that made friends with its identical twin in an airport en route to Florida, it only has small handles, no straps or large handles to tempt me to use it in any other way than in my hands. I am so glad I kept hold of it. (see what I did there!)

So, 23 sleeps. And counting

28th May 2014

Nervous about the pins and needles. I had my pre op   today. So many
questions, tests. needles. All in hospital. All very routine. Well, maybe, not
sure it is for me. The only thing that's routine here for me, is that I
routinely fill up with butterflies whenever I step foot in that hospital.

I have done that thing I used to do when it was time for bloods
throughout the toxic stuff. I have juiced like a crazy lady to make sure my
blood is good enough for the big day. Anyone wanting fennel in the
Shrewsbury area better get a move on as the stocks are depleting
fast.

Today, I have had to have a chat to myself. The picking up from the floor
type of chat. I am not having chemo in 3 weeks, those days are long gone.
I am, in fact, finishing this mammoth journey of mine. That is all good.
There is nothing bad in any of this. Well, apart from the actual operation
of course, more on that later, I will try and explain why it hurts so much,
as there is no way anyone would know unless, you know. And that's
exactly how it should be.

Funny, I still get a big quiver when I see cancer anywhere on TV. I can
busy myself like a demon to avoid such images or stories, she says writing
about it. Just as I was going to bed last night, an advert came on TV and
it started with a girl with blonde hair saying that when she could put her
hair in a pony tail again she was happy. I instantly knew it was
for   cancer. I knew because I often go to put mine in a pony tail and

when I can't, I remember. Not because I want a pony   tail, they didn't suit me when I had long hair, but I could then. I can't now. Maybe when my unruly curls get long enough I'll go pony tail mad. Because I can. If ever there was an advert about cancer research that I could ever feel ok about, it's this one. I do everything they do, I feel utter joy at the smallest of things, things I probably never even noticed before. I'm not going to get all romantic and emotional about the leaves on the trees and the sun in the sky, la, la la la la la la.. but trust me, its all pretty amazing.

So, I have just had a little glimmer of why I'm all at sea today. Great saying, thanks Dad, along with 'sick of the whole damn shooting match', I have used that one often! I wonder if he ever knew that I would use so many of his sayings with such gusto! Anyway, I am all at sea because I have to talk about all of this again. Put aside the actual operation, because that hurts. In fact, a quick operation description so you can see what I'm on about.

7 hours of surgery, muscle removed from back, through armpit to form the reconstruction with an implant, all breast tissue removed, nipples gone, skin graft from back   to reconstruct all stitched up, good to go. Recover. Nipples for Christmas.

Things I can't do after. Rock climbing and canoeing. Bugger! Oh, and if I want to take Miss Daisy on holiday, I can't carry the cases, not sure how to get around that one just yet. I think I'll be OK about the rock climbing and canoeing.

Anyway, I am all at sea. I have worked really hard searching for my new and improved 'something' and that has had me nicely focused on what wonders can be before me. The talking about what's been is only ok when it's on my terms. Selfish, perhaps, but it was me that went through all that, so I think that's fair enough.

Having to talk about it now, is because I am being prepared to go back and finish it. All the check ups, tests, questions from today, all the preparing to wind down work for a few weeks, all the not being able to drive, move, exercise, pick Miss Daisy up, and the list goes on. It all got to me.

But in true Jagger style, I got my focus back and remembered that I feel overwhelmingly grateful that I am here, to get all at sea about it.

22 sleeps and counting....

29th May 2014

So, today I had a moment. A very peculiar moment. It was a hair moment, but bare with me on that. I am, it is true, obsessed with my hair, I have been for 12 months. It was about that time, who am I kidding with 'about', it was exactly 1 year minus 12 days, that I had my 'Chanel moment' and had it chopped off ready for the inevitable to happen. Of course I defied inevitable and clung on as long as possible to the glorious blonde stuff.

Anyway, the reason for said hair obsession is,   it's the only visual part of me that has changed, apart from amazing skin, but I more or less look the same in every other way, give or take a couple of things, except my hair. So when it has gone

from long to short, fallen out, changed texture, grown back curly, it is the ever changing after effects of what has been.

Today, I was with the wondrous Miss Sally and all she said was she was going to dry my hair smooth and straighten it. I had an overwhelming feeling inside of 'me'. The me I thought I had lost. The straight haired, me. The me I didn't think I would see for some time to come.   I cried.   She did just as she said and I was there, looking back at myself in the mirror, all straight haired and me.

I cried.

It was a year ago today I was diagnosed with breast cancer for the second time.

A year, minus 12 days, and I have straight, thick, glorious hair. It will be curly again as soon as I wash it, I don't care. This was a big moment.

The magic of Miss Sally.   20 sleeps and counting.....

4th June 2014

So, Noah's ark rolled into Wem over the weekend, by Noah I mean my sister and Lou and their many animals and by ark, I of course mean their mammoth tent. It was a joy to have them stay, and I have clearly softened as I let them all in the house. Even Ness and Lou.

An odd thing happened though. My mum. I actually have no idea if she was odd, but that's beside the point, I found out more than I had before, about how much I am like her. I look like her, that bit is easy. But on so many occasions over the last few days I have been like her. Even through having cancer, it turns out we did similar things. Writing. Over and over again, nonsense, over and over again. For the first time, ever, I actually know how she felt about something. The power of cancer and what it does, different for everybody, but it seems me and my mum were the same. My dad never talked about her, he wanted to keep her memory close to his broken heart, but it was great to hear Ness talk about her, to enlighten me about a world I had let myself forget.

It's a funny thing, not particularly in the ha ha sense, but the 'really' sense, of how this has made me feel. Over and over in my head the words 'keep your face to the sunshine and you cannot see the shadows', the words mum wrote over and over again when she was ill. No doubt to keep herself going. I am, of course, the master of picking myself up from a very tricky floor, and I do this using very similar methods. Last year, I wrote, over and over, complete nonsense at particularly hard times, to keep myself going, to put the good back in my head, keep the fear at bay and the warmth back in my heart. I must have got this from her. Along with a love of walnut whips, with no walnuts. Of course.

Anyway, the other thing about this. I have had a very strong realisation that I really don't remember very much from her being alive, but I feel such a strong sense of love from that time. And that has been my pickle today. It's a hard love to replicate, a mother and daughter.

Today I have missed it. I, of course have it in bucket loads with Miss Daisy, but I missed a woman I can barely remember, but who I know made me feel like the most special person alive. It's a nice (ish) 'miss', and no doubt quite a necessary one.

So, I did the decent thing and distracted myself enough to power on through and ate a walnut whip. Without   the walnut.

14 sleeps and counting....

ps. I am happy that Ness reminded me of a lovely 'big love' feeling I had forgotten, I am happy that I am like that wonderful woman and very grateful I knew her at all and I am happy that I am me, still here, sharing my love for all things non walnut like...

8th June 2014

So, it seems my dad wanted in on the whole 'missing' action of a few days ago. In my dreams he has been hugging me and laughing with me and then he just got in his car and drove off. He must have felt left out, or he has forgiven me for not having carpets. Either way, all now is well with the whole missing of parents and I was very pleased to see that he was still driving his Jag. Clearly, it's all in the name.

Well, not even a walnut whip could make the world a better place today. I have declared a slight rebellion, I am well and truly sick of the whole damn shooting match and I am really, totally and utterly fed up with still having to do all this cancer stuff. All was going fine, well, apart from the mind numbing acceptance of the totally life changing'ness of the last 18 months. But fine as in I was doing all I could to make the absolute best of everything that was in front of me, and now I am heading deep into the world of what you have to have done to yourself to try and make sure it never comes back again, I don't like it much. In fact, there is nothing I like about it at all. Maybe, the life saving bit actually. Not the rest though.

So, I am just over a week away from surgery. I am preparing myself emotionally, physically and mentally. I am so bored of having to do this. This time last year I was doing the exact same thing but for the toxic stuff. 18 months ago I was doing the exact same things for being diagnosed. Miss impatient here is struggling with this today. I know all the positive stuff that relates to everything I am saying, today, it's just very well disguised. I am the queen of recovery and picking ones' self up from any floor, but I am so tired of doing so.

I have been working really hard on myself. Getting myself to a place where I feel good and happy with a future plan − a

vision of how I want my life to be. I have no idea yet how all my dreams will come true, but I at least know what my dreams are − that's a start. The one area of my life that's always been tricky - my relationships − I've always known a huge side effect from dead parents was a severe need to belong, I always just belonged to wrong somebody. I have dug deep about what this person is for me, their values, characteristics, desires, dreams, passions and I have concluded − this person does not exist. I will never compromise on this. Therefore, I am happy flying solo.

Now, when I say happy. I mean, on the whole I am. Just times like now, I really could do with someone cuddling me in the hours I lay awake at night full of fear.

Is it too early to go to bed at 6pm... I've cried a small ocean, I'm worn out, so no. Tomorrow is another day.   10 sleeps.

9th June 2014

I was in fact right, today has been another day, and with that brings a whole new pair of eyes to view the world   through. Phew.

Everyone around me has been waiting for me to come around to the fact that this surgery is super big and will be bringing back all sorts of nastiness in my head, they have just been waiting for me to see it myself. They have been nodding

with complete acceptance that the realisation is a good thing, better out than in and all that. I, on the other hand, have been super frustrated at my lack of control over my own emotional state.

And there it is. Again.

The struggle between me, and, well, me.   I am my own worst enemy, critic, pain in the ass. I am again trying to do everything all at the same time. Get over the getting over of the big C, big surgery, again, selling house, again, and the general re focusing, re prioritising re everything. I believe this is called distraction and the biggest need in the world to move on. I am doing both, quite successfully. Sometimes I just don't see it. Just like I don't see how big it has all been, until days like yesterday.

The good that comes out of days like yesterday are immense. The good that comes out of every day actually, but maybe I just tune in more when I'm in despair. Its all about the people. The love and care people show, probably without really realising it, does something quite magical. Bright rainbows, 10k runs, boxing gloves, dragons, swords and the ones who got me through all the pickles of the past. And of course, Miss Daisy. See, there's magic, real life magic.

Anyway, I may just have to accept this week might be a bit wobbly. I can cope, I just forget sometimes.

9 sleeps....

<u>15th June 2014</u>

So, my wibbly wobbly path this week has led me to today. I have quite successfully become the queen of distraction once again. No bad thing. There is a time and a place for just being. This is not the time, or the place. I can cry at any given moment, stop at any given moment, and have no idea when these particular moments are going to present themselves. Not much control going on here I can tell you, and for those that know me, this is not a good thing. These tears, however, are full of the pain of what's been and the joy of what's coming with a whole load of nerves thrown in for good measure.

So, I finished work for a few weeks on Friday. Again. It was a day full of walnut whips, boxes of them, and my obligatory argument with AXA. Will they pay, won't they pay, how much will they make me cry before realising it was all agreed last year, you know the sort of thing. It was those lovely people at work, and the walnut whips, but mainly the people, who kept me going, as they have many times before, without even knowing it.

I put my out of office on and got in my car a big mixed bag of emotion. Full of fear, happiness, pending relief, confused excitement and a lot of impatience. I just want to get to the end of this. The big C has held me hostage for so long. 18

months. It's all in the timing, apparently. This time last year I was in the toxic zone. I was preparing for the treatment of all treatments. My hair had just gone and I was heading into the unknown. The good news is, I arrived. I am here. Everything I have been doing over the last 18 months has been to save my life. Its taken me this long to realise it's all been worth the pain, and boy has it hurt at times.

So this last bit, is just that, the last bit, my final bid for safety.

That feeling of elation I have been banging on about, the one that I thought I would feel and never actually have, is close. It is heading my way, really heading my way. I believe it will find a very drugged up girl in a hospital bed at around 4pm on Wednesday.

3 sleeps...

17th June 2014

Well, here I am, the night before the big day. Nervous.

Alex Jagger

So, today has been about bikini waxes, short buying, nice smelling skin stuff, feet, cleaning and   crying. Normal behaviour for someone going on holiday maybe, apart from the crying, of course. But for me, it seems it is completely normal behaviour for someone who is about to become the bionic woman.

It has also been about those pesky tears of whatever they are full of. The heart ache of saying goodbye to Miss Daisy this evening or the big, massive butterflies that refuse to do anything but, well, flutter. But then on the flip side, in- between waxing and crying, it has been full of the joy of discarding the burden of cancer for the final time.

And of course, it has been all about the people, those lovely, lovely, lovely people, helping me remember all is actually wonderful.

So, here goes....

22th June 2014

There is no place like home. It has to be said. With 3 clicks of my very sparkly heels I am miraculously here. Well, when I say with 3 clicks, I actually mean with every single ounce of everything I have and a lot of what I didn't know I had, and when I say miraculously, I mean just that. It's a miracle that I got to this point today. But there it is, I am miraculously here with all the miracles in the universe and it is an absolute joy. It also hurts like hell, but that's just a formality.

So, I am here, at home and feeling, well, just feeling. I would like to say that I was feeling over the moon, relieved, over joyed and all that goes along with it, from the minute I came round. I am sure I did, but I think the morphine was doing   the talking then. In fact, the morphine did a lot of talking and kept me very busy in a twirly wirly state of mind. That was until around 8am yesterday.

Yesterdays view out of my window was glorious, as was the feeling of contentment within me. I have made it. I have done it. I am a curly haired wonder, full of bionicness, bandages, bruises, and drains, but, magically, a very happy one.

Me and my sparkly heels are off to recover, to protect this new body of mine and this new found wonder that's ingrained within every tiny part of me. It's magic.

27th June 2014

So, I now know why I haven't been able to sleep. Apart from the obvious new bionic'ness that's going on, of course, and the almighty wound that spans half my back. My insomnia is all about the drain. Sounds obvious I know. The drain that,   I naively believed, was just inside my skin. Well, yes, it   was. All 12 inches of it. Oh boy, I had such a shock when it came out today, when I saw how much plastic was pressing on the inside of my back. And then it all made sense. And then I realised that of course it had to be so blooming long to do its job. And then I realised I might actually get some sleep tonight.

So, one week on and I'm doing everything I should be   doing. Nothing. If I don't move too much all is well. This is, of course, super boring for Miss Daisy. She is so over me being ill. She asked me to play catch with her the day I came out of hospital. Tricky. Luckily Nessa has been here to play catch, you're the best, you're the worst, la la la la game, hoola hooping, trampolining, and list goes on of things I can't do, Dave has been doing a splendid meals on wheels' service and my house has become a temporary florist. All in the name of recovery.

And recovering is just what I am doing. I am climbing over the emotional hump of breaking the cycle. The cycle of thinking the sky is gong to fall in, the world is going to end, the results next week will be bad, I'll have to go through this all over again, that fear and recovery rule me. Sounds crazy, I know. Maybe it's the drugs, but I've had a funny few days feeling a bit stuck in time. Off work, sore as hell, feel sick when I move, mountains of drugs to take, sore veins. I feel easily led, easily fooled, like someone has got one over on me.

This is the cycle I am breaking. Broken. Nearly broken.   I secretly know the future is bright for me and Miss Daisy,   I just need to tell myself it's not a secret anymore.   I have to remember that I was the girl who was making the nurses walk around the hospital car park with me at the weekend when

others hadn't even made it out of bed. So determined was I to recover in style. I have to remember I've got this. I am blooming amazing to have got this far – on my own whilst keeping Miss Daisy's sunshine fully intact. This is the secret I'm doing a great job keeping from myself.

Anyway, nothing a good curly hair chat couldn't sort out. I'm going to give sleeping a go, minus the plastic.

<u>29th June 2014</u>

So, this time last week I was dragging a ridiculous amount of plastic tubing around with me whilst feeling every single little ache and pain, with every stitch, bruise and swollen bit. Wondering how on earth I was going to get any sleep with all that going on, along with my new found bionic'ness. Well, what a difference a week makes.

A week of clever clogs surgeons, being freed of all my dressings and having Miss Daisy home again has been the name of the game. And possibly over doing it a little. Well, over doing it a lot and being banished to bed with Miss Daisy to suffer the consequences. Now that is no bad thing. Nine days from the slicing and dicing and not one of those with any sleep, the first time Miss Daisy was wrapped around me, out like a light. Absolutely perfect.

So, my clever clogs surgeon, Dan the boob man, was super happy with me. I managed a whole conversation with him for

about 20 minutes stood up, naked from the waste up, and it felt completely normal. I so have a crush on him. Not the normal type of crush, you know, the dreamy type, no, this is the man who is giving me back my body. He's not quite done, but so far, so blooming good. I have an equally big crush on my other surgeon. He fixed me and took away the   nasty's. One takes it all away as the other one rebuilds me. See, clever clogs. They must get that a lot.   There is nothing better, right now, than being told, by   my crush, that all is looking good.

Results this week. Logic says they are good. My head is staging a fairly good argument against that. Let the battle commence.

So, here's to happy. Big, fat, wonderful happy. And nipples. That's all I'm missing.

<u>2nd July 2014</u>

So then, my results are in. My last results. The results that have kept me awake for the last 2 weeks. The results that have provoked one almighty battle between logic, reason and my old friend, emotion. The results that have had me mentally preparing for another trip with the toxic stuff, for a never ending cycle of results, results and more results.

Well, the cycle has been broken. I am CLEAR of the dreaded Big C.

C. ancer free

L. ife begins again

E very bit of me is cancer free

A bsolutely all of me

R idiculously happy

That is what I thought up in the waiting room. Seems only right to use it.

So, I cried as soon as I saw my surgeon, I cried when he put his hand on my back, and for a very long moment I thought I was doomed. I cried when he finally told me all was good. I say cry, I sobbed. Poor man. He must get that a lot. I cried when he told me he didn't need to see me for 6 months, for my, now, regular check up. That sounded like music to my ears. Regular check up. How wonderful.

I cried when he told me I am healing really well, I cried when he gave me a hug before I left and I cried, well, I just cried.

All with joy. Beautiful, cancer free, joy.

14th July 2014

So, this has been my story (again). I have been a little speechless at how to say, what I wanted to say, on this day.

The last 18 months have brought many a speechless moment, along with a flow of words that needed to be said, to get me to here. I have shared my pain, fear, joy, the bits that I've lost and the bits that I've gained and my many toxic   stories. Seems it's a bit of a long drawn out thing, this cancer stuff. Not the actual cancer, as that's long gone, but all that goes with it.

I have puzzled over people's welcome return to what they were, after taking a walk with the big C. I wondered in amazement how it was remotely possible to be that person, to want to fall back into what was once normal. I am amazed no more. I can truly see why normal life calls, lulls you in when you least expect it, catching you off guard. Same old, same old looks surprisingly tempting at times.

And that's where the problem lies. Of course, I made a promise to myself whilst high as a kite on various levels of the toxic'ness and possibly whilst going under or coming round from various anesthetics, that I would learn from what I have been through. That I would not resume where I had left off. I would learn to overcome my fears and learn to love the girl that I found. That girl is me. Alex Jagger, life long companion to Miss Daisy and all those lovely people I've talked about for the last 18 months, and anyone else who may come my way. I made a promise to live. Really live. To

go after every single thing I could and make it happen. I made a promise to do what I say I am going to do, or just not say it, and to break the cycle. The cycle, any cycle, of not changing what needs to be changed when it needs to be changed. All in a good way.

Easier said than done. But a promise is a promise. A cancer fuelled promise is even more potent. It means there is no backing out, no going back on that word, no changing my mind. That is also easier said than done. It's a funny limbo land of not quite there but can't turn back. Same old, same old is calling out and is looking mighty fine, but new and exciting and sticking to my promise is ahead, but I just can't quite see all of it. Little shiny glimmers flash before my eyes and tiny sparkly bits fall on my shoulders. I'm so close I can almost feel it. I might even be here, I just don't recognise it yet as it's all new.

So, I'm at that amazing point of no return. Phew. It's been one hell of a journey getting here. Just when I thought the tricky bit was over. No! Turns out that was just the physical and obvious emotional trickiness. No one mentioned the crash and burn of the looking back and trying to learn all those many lessons that came my way. It takes as long as it takes, the good news is I'm doing it, feeling it and being me throughout it.

Now, this is not bad. This is just part of it. And now I am past

the point of no return I am feeling good, as I know I will not go back. I can't go back. That me, reminds me of being   ill. This me, the one who was swimming today, four weeks after a mastectomy and reconstruction, is the one I'm keen on keeping.

Today, I smiled all day at getting into that swimming pool and trying to swim. I swam. Slowly, very slowly, but I swam.

So, whilst swimming through all that glittery water, I felt the strongest need yet to finish this chapter in my life. I have the glorious chance to move on, all fully reformed. Well, nearly. I still have 2 more skin grafts and 2 tattoos to make up what apparently will look amazing. I believe that's called a silver lining........

Anyway, I have a glorious chance to move on with a new perspective. I was always a straight taking, hard working, determined thing. I am now more so, and have learned to overcome things I've wanted to overcome for years, and a few things I didn't even know were there.

A bit of a cliché, but I feel free and more alive than I ever have. How ironic, that cancer, the thing that I feared the most, along with the sky falling in, is the thing that has saved me. I would not recommend my methods, I'm sure there are

other ways, if needed, just like there are other ways to get good skin. Clarins. NOT chemotherapy. My skin does still glow, not sure if that's the radiation or just the rejuvenated me.

So, I have my lists. I have my health. I have my promises. I have my new bionic'ness. I have my lessons. I have Miss Daisy. I have my life long companions. I have me. I have a future. I have dreams I want to make realities. I have people I have yet to meet. I also have some more recovering to do.

Thank you for sharing in my journey and helping me find the girl with the big smile, the girl who can call herself a cancer survivor, the girl who see's all the possibilities and the girl who never breaks a promise. That girl is me.

Now, that's what I call rock and roll, of the very, very best kind!

8th July 2015

One Year Later……..

So, what happened next?

A year on from the end of a big, scary fight with the big C, being rebuilt from the inside out physically and emotionally and ready to take on the world, what has happened to the girl who found her smile?

Well, I am still that girl. Alex Jagger. I am healthy. I am fully reconstructed, Dan the boob man certainly worked his magic. My last stay in hospital was last October. I thought nipples would be easy, turned out I was wrong. I am and always will be the life long companions of Miss Daisy and many of the people I talked about over the last two and a half years. I have lived life to my new set of rules and have never forgotten how I got to today, for all the right reasons.

And, most importantly, I have just made the biggest, life changing decision I made since declining chemotherapy the first time the big C came to visit. That back then probably saved my life. I believe this decision is about to do the same in a completely different way.

So, let me explain. I wanted to tell the end of the story, or the beginning of the story, depends how you want to look at it. This is the art of the possible I dreamed about whilst arguing with the toxic nonsense, the courage I knew I still had in reserve and the power of believing the sky holds no limits. I had cancer. I thought my life was over, I was wrong. On this occasion that's a good thing. I was in a protected world of recovery, health, fennel and lovely people helping me.

I listened to my promises, defined my non negotiables and the areas of my life that were not up for compromise and decided, in detail, what and who I wanted to share in my journey, making every effort to remove all those limiting beliefs I had once lived my life by. Of course, all this was done in the comfort of my own world, my own little bubble of happiness and joy of just being alive, and giving it all I'd got, as I had promised to myself to do. Life was good because I had made it so. And because I had chosen life and happiness, amazing things started to happen.

I landed my dream job in August last year, in the company I had worked at since I was 24. The job amazingly directly related to my Masters Degree (distinction remember) always a bonus. I landed this dream job because I pitched for it whilst recovering from mastectomy no.2. As part of my big life plan I had made a set of decisions around my career and then – serendipity maybe – the job I wanted came free. I did what any girl worth her salt would do – I went for it. And. I got it.

I worked hard, I took action and I put my passion into it. I did this whilst recovering from the numerous surgeries that followed to finish off my reconstruction. Two small but very significant and blooming painful finishing touches later and all was looking good, on my front and the job front. I did a pretty good job of keeping all the surgery nonsense and toxic side effects at bay whilst getting on and doing a cracking job at work.

So - that big decision, the biggest one I have made since that heart breaking chemo day in 2013. Well, after landing my dream job and loving every working moment of it, I discovered something I really hadn't expected, but something

truly amazing. Or should I say someone. Now this came out of nowhere, but I believe it always does.

My news years' resolution for 2015 was to be done with nonsense, to be swept off my feet by that man in my head, you know the one that doesn't actually exist and to drink more of the sparkly stuff, more on the sparkly stuff later, but the being swept off my feet thing actually came true. And remember, I am different and my body is different, those two very important factors had lead me to believe I would never find someone who would see through my scars and get the life I wanted to lead.

I actually believed the man I wanted didn't exist. I had written about this man, I had lists about him, his values, dreams and ideas and everything that I would never compromise on. Through all of my coaching, a big part was understanding the kind of man I wanted – not needed – but really wanted.

I had accepted he did not exist. I was far happier in my own relationship with myself than to even consider compromising any more for someone who wasn't right.

I was wrong. Again. Hallelujah!

Seems being wrong really isn't so bad. Seems that exactly two years on from that fateful February day when I declined

a possible life saving treatment, for all the right, well calculated reasons, a new door was opening up right in front of my very eyes. So, this is the part where I get truly dreamy. This is the bit where I say, in as few a words as I can, what has happened. So, here goes;

He doesn't see my scars he only sees me. He has brought a kind of sunshine into my life that I did not know existed anywhere apart from in my dreams, there is adventure and mischief, we think alike, we have challenge and passion in equal amount that dominate our endless conversations; funny excitement and laughter flow and the art of the possible is the art of making it happen. Care, reciprocation, trust, belief and an absolute certainty that we will go all out to make our dreams come true together.

Who knew all that even existed? Not me. Until now. I know why people write about this stuff, it really is something   else. I met that man - the one I made up in my head – who'd have thought it, just goes to show what can happen when you get some clarity. We'd known each other for months. I'd got over the two-year mark, thought enough was enough and decided to categorically leave the cancer world behind me. It allowed me to see though my own eyes again and look at what was right in front of me. The flood gates opened to a new life. The planets were clearly aligned as we were both in the right place at exactly the right time.

My big decision, well, there was only ever going to be one man who can bring so much sunshine to my life, but there are going to many other dream jobs, so me and that dream job parted company. After 20 years. It was the job that I always thought was my crutch in life, the one constant and I was letting it go. When you know, you know. There is no point in messing with time when time is the one with the upper hand. I figured it was time to live.

So, the doors to a new world are opening up again. I am taking a leap of faith in my career and doing something I have longed to do. Without sounding too clichéd, I believe I am living the dream. My dream to be precise. Of course, this dream can feel quite scary at times, but isn't it the fear of the unknown that transforms into the art of the possible that breathes life into uncertainty? I think so. However, the new doors that have opened are not all about my career, that's part of removing all those self limiting beliefs that once ruled me.

We have a life. I have sunshine in the form of the life long companions in Mr. D and Miss Daisy. We have a crazy dog that brings utter chaos and jumpy joy to our world. We have truly amazing friendships, that are only about love, understanding and mutual support, fun and kindness whether that's every day, week or year, this sort of friendship does not fail. I have lots and lots of time ahead of me as a healthy

person, I run, I walk, I swim in crystal, magical water that makes me feel alive, I juice daily, I have sparkly stuff to drink, places to see, people still to meet and I have dreams to fulfil. And WE are doing all of this together.

You know me and promises.

Watch out world, I am ready, willing and more than able to knock your socks off.

Here's to remembering the joy of soapy shampoo.

<u>May 2016</u>

Three years later.......
So, three years from being diagnosed for a second time with breast cancer.

What happened next?

After finding my mojo along with the man I never thought existed, life is pretty amazing. Miss Daisy is now eight, she has doubled in age since I was ill and she talks about it now as much as she's ever done. It's very clear for children, it's far from over even when the last stitch is sown into my body. She is bright and full of sunshine and the joys of life. We have written a book together. More on that later.
I am not the girl who started this journey. I have worked my socks off to be the girl I am today. I am full of joy and wonder and sunshine of the very brightest kind. I have learnt how to keep my face to the sunshine and to never hide in the shadows again.

I was in search of something that felt illusive. I had a head full of dreams and fears, in equal measure, about what I wanted my future to look like. I needed to make sense of them before they drove me mad! It seemed there was nobody out there right for me to help un-jumble my vision for my future. By sheer chance I stumbled across a coach and mentor who fit the bill. The Joyous Jessica. At last! The work we did together changed my life again, but this time for all the right reasons.
I felt so strongly about my coaching and the way the joyous Jessica helped unlock my mind that I decided to retrain myself so I could do the same for other people. The student became the teacher and I have been lucky enough to help people, who, like me couldn't find what they were looking for.
I didn't want pity; I knew why I was in a pickle. I wanted someone to help me sort out my emotions, work out why I couldn't cope with the relief, push the past away and focus on the future. My life had changed. I was still the professional woman I was when it started, I was still a mother and still a friend but I barely recognized anything else.

The focus for my coaching I now offer is a guide for people through their journey. I believe that once you can know what makes your heart sing you stand a much better chance of working out how to get there.

If you feel like me and the people I have coached, I'd love to hear from you. You can book a discovery session with me to help you though your journey, or you can leave your email address on my website for access to a private Facebook group for 'in the moment' support – safe in the knowledge you are among like minded people who get it and know a trick or two to get you back on your feet again. You catch up on my blog about life, in all it's wonder whilst you're there.

Check out my website www.alexjagger.com. It would be wonderful to hear from you. You may notice I've taken my shoe analogy to new heights!!

Talking of shoes, Miss Daisy's first word was 'shoes" (girl after my own heart clearly). And talking of books and Miss Daisy, we have written one together. Telling Daisy I had cancer was one of the hardest things I have ever had to do. It makes my heart ache still when I think about it.

I looked everywhere for books to help me. I found nothing that suited me and her. Therefore, I did it my own way and she hers, with the help of her dad, Dave. We have both come out of this in good shape and I want to tell people how we did it. Our book "Amazing Daysies" will be out soon. It's her story told through her eyes written with my help and perspective. It is practical as it is truthful. It is as relevant today for us as it was when I was diagnosed. We have all come out smiling, and we know there is a life that is amazing because we are already living it. Shoes, life, love and sunshine await.........

With Love

Thank you. From the bottom of my heart. To all those that helped me on this crazy journey and for all those that have read my story. Please pass this book on to someone else. It could make all the difference.

To Miss Daisy – life would be unbelievably dull without this ray of sunshine. She's one amazing girl. I am blessed for such an amazing daughter.

To Alistair – my sunshine. You believe in every inch of me. You make me feel like the best girl in the world. I am very lucky.

To all my friends – you're all fab!

To my family – thank you Nessa for driving across the country to be with me in my hours of need and for Claudia for providing medical equipment for Daisy to feel the part.

About The Author

I was born in Yorkshire in 1970. I had the happiest of childhoods with my two sisters, Vanessa and Claudia, my mum, a famous author, and my dad who claimed to hold the world together. He manufactured nuts and bolts so in a way he did. At fifteen mum died of cancer. This devastated our family. Whilst the world was going mad around us, I managed to get myself through school and University.

I fell into a job after I graduated which turned out to be the start of a great career. It was in the pub industry. My dad couldn't believe his luck. Whilst working my socks off making sure beer was being sold in abundance, I studied for a Masters Degree in Leadership and Social Engagement and I trained to become a Coach. All was going well.

In 2013 I was diagnosed with breast cancer twice – the world changed all over again.

I am now a writer and coach. I guide my clients through life changing circumstances – in search of what truly makes their heart sing. I found myself in no mans land stuck in-between my old life that was fraught with disaster and a new life I thought I could only dream of. With the help of my coach I made my dreams a reality, in my career, in love and in motherhood. I am now guiding people to that very special place that makes them smile. I founded "Coaching Girl" in March 2106.

Connect with me, I'd love to hear from you:
www.alexjagger.com
www.coachinggirl.com
Twitter @coachinggirl
Instagram italljustrocknroll
thecoachinggirl

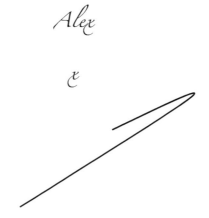

Alex

x

17382091R00172

Printed in Poland
by Amazon Fulfillment
Poland Sp. z o.o., Wrocław